DAVID,

A MAN AFTER THE HEART OF GOD

Lessons From the Life of David

BY THEODORE H. EPP

Founder and Director
of Back to the Bible Broadcast

A BACK TO THE BIBLE Publication

$1.50 each

order from

BACK TO THE BIBLE BROADCAST
Lincoln, Nebraska 68501

37,000 printed to date—1969
(5-9389—3M—129)

Printed in the United States of America

Foreword

David, Israel's great king, was an outstanding man in many ways. The studies in this book follow him from youth to old age with this question uppermost: What made David a man after God's own heart? It is this side of David's life that helps to explain why he was outstanding as a military strategist, prophet, psalm writer, king and above all as a humble believer in the Lord.

These messages were given over the international network of the Back to the Bible Broadcast. So great was the impact on Christians who saw in David a "man of like passions" whose spiritual problems and experiences paralleled their own, that we received hundreds of requests for the messages to be published. We decided to do this; and though it makes a much larger book than we ordinarily print, it has the decided advantage of keeping together this comprehensive treatment of the Christian's walk and spiritual warfare as seen in the experiences of David.

To discover the relationship of many of the Davidic Psalms with David's personal history was also a source of real joy to many radio listeners. The Psalms have taken on new significance since it has become clear that they are rooted in history and heart experiences. References are made to this all through the messages, and a section is added at the end of the book which summarizes this phase of the studies.

We trust the spiritual enrichment which came to many hearts through these radio messages will continue as this book carries them in printed form into the homes and lives of God's people.

—John I. Paton
Literature Editor

CONTENTS

CHAPTER ONE

CHOOSING A KING

David, son of Jesse, a member of the Tribe of Judah, was Israel's second king, not her first. In his patriarchal blessing, Jacob predicted that Judah would be preeminent among the tribes of Israel (Gen. 49:8-12). But the nation of Israel in Samuel's day was not willing to wait for either God's best time or God's best man. Saul, a member of the tribe of Benjamin, was chosen to be Israel's first king. Though he appeared to be all that men might desire in a leader, he was a failure from God's standpoint.

Saul was handsome, a man of commanding appearance, strong and so tall that he stood head and shoulders above his people. He must have been a man of magnetic personality because the people took to him readily, and Samuel the prophet had a high regard for him. In fact, when in his second year of reigning Saul showed himself unfitted for the responsibilities of the kingship, Samuel was grieved to see Saul rejected and another put in his place.

When Samuel was sent to the house of Jesse to anoint one of his sons to be king, the old prophet apparently assumed that since Saul was a man of striking physical appearance God would choose another like him. As Eliab, Jesse's oldest son, stood before him, Samuel said in his heart, "Surely the Lord's anointed is before him." It was then God showed Samuel that the divine standard was not according to a man's physical appearance but according to his heart attitude toward God.

"Look not on his countenance," the Lord said, "or on the height of his stature; because I have refused him: for the Lord seeth not as man seeth; for man looketh on the outward appearance, but the Lord looketh on the heart" (I Sam. 16:7).

It was to this fact that Paul referred when he said in Acts 13:22,23: "And when he [God] had removed him [Saul], he raised up unto them David to be their king; to whom also he gave testimony, and said, I have found David the son of Jesse, a man after mine own heart, which shall fulfill all my will. Of this man's seed hath God according to his promise raised unto Israel a Saviour, Jesus." So then, God's choice was a heart choice. It is clear from this that God's thoughts are not our thoughts, and our ways are not God's ways (Isa. 55:8,9). God looked for a man whose heart was right toward Him and found him in David.

In spite of David's imperfections—and they were many—two excellent qualities stand out concerning him: he cast himself upon God's mercy, and he trusted God implicitly. He was a man who put God's will ahead of his own selfish desires. In the main, David's life was a life of obedience to the will of God. There were times when he failed, but when he did, he turned again in repentance and threw himself on God's mercy. David's heart was fixed to do the will of God (Ps. 57:7), and because of this God made a covenant with him in which the kingdom of David was established forever. God said, "I have made a covenant with my chosen, I have sworn unto David my servant, Thy seed will I establish forever, and build up thy throne to all generations" (Ps. 89:3,4).

Some of the contrasts between Saul and David are too obvious to be overlooked as we take up this study of the man after God's own heart. Saul in his carnality either thought that God did not mean what He said about removing him as King, or else he foolishly thought he could thwart the purposes of God by destroying the person God had chosen in his place. How futile all these plans proved to be. First of all, Saul called David into his presence and gave him training for leadership, not knowing David was to be his successor. The moods of madness which came upon Saul as he allowed vindictive plans to ferment in his mind and heart were soothed away by the skillful harp playing of David who, while he knew he was to be Israel's next sovereign, did nothing to harm Saul. At the same time David learned court life and some of the responsibilities of government.

It is very likely in the first years following David's anointing as king only Samuel and Jesse and his sons knew of that choice. Yet David's place in his own family was a lowly one, for he had the menial task of herding his father's sheep. In the better-to-do families servants were called on to watch the sheep, but in Jesse's family where there were eight sons the youngest was given this lowly task. Nevertheless, under God's direction, that early training had real significance. From Psalm 78 we learn that God "chose David also his servant, and took him from the sheepfolds: From following the ewes great with young he brought him to feed Jacob his people, and Israel his inheritance" (vv. 70,71).

This, however, is in keeping with God's way of doing things, for we read in I Corinthians 1:26: "For ye see your calling, brethren, how that not many wise men after the flesh, not many mighty, not many noble, are called: But God hath chosen the foolish things of the world to confound the wise." Another translation has it: "God hath chosen that which the world counts foolish to confound the wisdom of the world. God hath chosen what the world counts weak in order to confound the things mighty of the world—the base things of the world, the things that are despised, God chose, yea, the things which are not, as far as the world is concerned, to bring to nought the things that are: that no flesh should glory in His presence."

David's difference in character from that of Saul was a great deal more than just the difference in human disposition. The Spirit of the Lord came upon David on the day of His anointing and remained with him (I Sam. 16:13). It is to David's obedience to the Spirit of God that his great contributions to his generations and ours are to be attributed. At least half of the Psalms were written by David, and the high character of his life which distinguished him from Saul was due to the divine life in Him.

Even as a youth David was recognized for his outstanding abilities. When Saul's depressed moods fell upon him, he sought for someone who could help lift his unhappy spirits. One of his servants recommended David in these words: "Behold, I have seen a son of Jesse the Bethlehemite, that is cunning in playing, and a mighty valiant man, and a man of war, and prudent in matters, and a comely person, and the Lord is with him" (I Sam. 16:18). What a reputation is this! David was a gifted musician, a man to be counted on in trouble and a tried warrior. He was good to look upon, was intelligent in his speech and best of all, "the Lord was with him."

Saul wasted no time in sending messengers to Jesse with a demand that David, who was with the sheep, be sent to Saul's court. Jesse had no alternative. He had to obey. As an Oriental King, Saul's power and authority was supreme.

From here on out as we trace David's life, we will see the things that made him great and also the places where he was tripped up by the enemy. In it all, we will gather practical lessons for our own lives, lessons which down through the years have become increasingly helpful in my own spiritual life.

We will see David's conduct and attitude toward Saul and how wisely David behaved himself. He made no claims for the throne. He would not raise his hand against God's anointed but left everything with God.

The members of his own family were not always cordial toward him, and yet he was always gracious in his treatment of them. Many of the Psalms came out of these bitter waters through which David passed, and these inspired hymns have been repeating their messages to every generation of believers from that time on. Let us ask God to open up this mine of spiritual instruction in the life of David that we might gather riches to adorn the gospel of Christ in our own lives through hearts wholly submitted to God and showing implicit trust in Him.

I Am Resolved

I am resolved no longer to linger,
Charmed by the world's delight.
Things that are higher, things that are nobler,
These have allured my sight.

I am resolved to follow the Saviour,
Faithful and true each day;
Heed what He sayeth, do what He willeth,
He is the Living Way.

CHAPTER TWO

EARLY TESTS AND TRIUMPHS

I Samuel 16,17

Having been anointed to be king of Israel, David's life could never be the simple life of a shepherd boy again. He was able to return to his flocks for brief periods, but those times soon ceased. As Psalm 23 indicates, the personal knowledge of his Shepherd never was altogether lost to David. The reminders of the Lord's majesty and care and the benefits of the quiet pastures and still waters steadied David in many a crisis. And they helped bring about the restoration of his soul when he sinned.

Such was the quality of David's life that when he first appeared at the royal residence, Saul "loved him greatly" (I Sam. 16:21,22). David came to dispell with his sweet music, the evil spirit that often fell upon Saul. He, of course, did not know that David was to be his successor. On the other hand, David behaved so well, and was so humble that Saul had no reason to dislike him, but rather to admire and love him. He made David his armor-bearer and sent word to Jesse that his son was now attached to the inner circle of the king's bodyguard.

Shortly after this the Philistines gathered their armies together and came against Israel. Jesse's three oldest sons joined the army of Israel in order to help repel the invaders. This apparently also changed the work of David so that he was able to go home at intervals and attend to his father's sheep. Verse 15 of I Samuel 17 says, "But David went and returned from Saul to feed his father's sheep at Beth-lehem." A more exact translation has it that David went back and forth between Saul and the sheep herding. When Saul's dark mood would come upon him, he would send for David; then when the evil spirit was repelled, David would return again to his home.

Consider what this meant to David. While appearing before Saul, David held a position of honor and prominence, but back home he did the work of a servant. Whether in prominence or lowliness, however, David's attitude was a healthy spiritual one of humility. Could we do the same under similar conditions? What would be our reaction to being exalted on the one hand and being called on for very menial tasks on the other?

In contrast to David's attitude is that of his oldest brother. No doubt, Eliab was not pleased when he was turned down and David was chosen to be anointed as king. Eliab's physical appearance appealed strongly to Samuel, but his disposition, at least at this time in his life, was in poor contrast to that of his youngest brother. Eliab, too, when with Saul was only a common soldier. That, however, was enough to make him proud and to chide and rebuke David and accuse him of pride when he came to visit the Israelite army. Still there is no record that David ever held this against his brother.

We have anticipated a little history here, but it fits into the practical lesson suggested by the portion of Scripture under consideration. We turn back now to this situation that developed when the Philistines came against the Israelites. Their armies were drawn up against each other "army against army" (v. 21), and it was at this very time that God saw to it that David was sent to visit his brothers. God always times things right.

God had found in David a man who would do his bidding. David knew his God in a personal way and knew His power. He made this quite plain to Saul when he described his fighting with a lion and a bear. Such odds were too great for any young man, even as great a warrior as was David, but with God's strength he overcame.

How different was David's vision from that of Israel's. Goliath, the champion of the Philistines, would stand between the two armies and defy any Israelite, including Saul, to fight him; and at the same time he defied God. But apparently Goliath was all that the Israelites saw. Their vision did not go beyond the vain glory of that man who defied them and frightened them.

David's reaction was very different. The first time he heard Goliath's challenge David realized that Goliath was not only defying Israel's army but the living God, also. David's eyes were on God and his heart was stirred within him at the blasphemous utterances of the giant Philistine. What is our first concern? Is it for ourselves or for the church or for the Lord? Paul's great desire was to know Christ and the power of His resurrection. Is this our desire also?

David and Eliab

Though David had been sent by his father to take food to his brothers, they did not receive him cordially. When Eliab, his eldest brother, heard him asking some of the soldiers what would be done for the man who would destroy the Philistine and take away the reproach from Israel, Eliab lost his temper. He said, "Why camest thou down hither? and with whom hast thou left those few sheep in the wilderness? I know thy pride, and the naughtiness of thine heart; for thou art come down that thou mightest see the battle" (v. 28).

David's answer was two questions: "What have I now done? Is there not a cause?" (v. 29). Was not God being defamed? Was not the God of Israel being shamed before the two armies? Was not the God of Abraham, Isaac and Jacob being belittled before the unbelieving Philistines and before His own people? David was asking his brother if he could conscientiously tolerate God's Name being dragged in the mud and not do something about it—"Is there not a cause?" David believed rightly that there was.

We cannot be too sure of David's age at this time, but very likely he was in his early twenties. Though he was only beginning to come into manhood physically, he had a spiritual maturity far beyond that of many of his contemporaries. This was why when the Israelites fled in fear before the advancing Goliath, David, because he knew his God, did not run. Even believers will find themselves in situations where their hearts will quail in fear simply because their personal knowledge of God is not adequate.

This is the situation in the world today. There is great fear among the nations, and even Christians are affected by it. We see Communism taking over vast territories and great populations, and we wonder how long this can last and if the whole world will not soon be under the Communist heel. Men stand in fear just as the Bible said they would in the last days. Governments and nations are filled with fear as they see the things that are coming on the earth. There is one thing that we Christians can be sure of, however, God is the Master of time and of the boundaries of the nations. He will bring matters to a head and to an end in accordance with His prearranged plans. It might be well for us to read often the Book of the Revelation, for there we see God's hand among the nations in the last days. There He is revealed as Master of the whole world situation.

God has not given us the spirit of fear but of a sound mind, as we read in II Timothy 1:7. David showed this quality of divine life in his day when most of Saul's army was ready to panic and run.

David did not quail before Goliath and his boastings. The future king of Israel asked, "Who is this uncircumcised Philistine that dares defy the armies of the living God?" David had courage, a courage based on his knowledge of God. He had an unspoiled reverence for Almighty God. He believed that no one was strong enough to defy God. To see Israel reproached by this evil being was to David an insult to his people and to his God. Recognizing also that God had been defied, David decided something had to be done.

It was about this time that David's oldest brother accosted him and accused him of pride. The Scripture tells us that Eliab's anger was kindled against David which is understandable enough from the human standpoint. He had been set aside while David had been anointed to be the future king of Israel. Of course, no one would tell Saul that, not even Eliab, for in that case, Saul would possibly have killed the whole family as being a threat to his ambitions.

Eliab did not stop with being angry, he belittled David. He asked him, "With whom did you leave those few sheep?" David was hardly even considered a member of the family in some respects. When Samuel came to the household of Jesse, the seven brothers of David were brought before Samuel, but David was left with the sheep. It was almost as though he was not considered a member of the family. We do not know why this was, but part of it could have been due to David's being very conscious of Almighty God, and this may have angered his relatives. Eliab said that he knew all about the naughtiness of David's heart, but he did not. Had he known the heart of David, he would have known that David was a man after the heart of God. He accused David of coming down to see the battle, but there was no battle to be seen. The Israelites were afraid to go into battle against Goliath. Eliab's berating of David was totally unfair, and his accusations against David had no foundation in fact.

We must remember that according to II Timothy 3:12 "All that will live godly in Christ Jesus shall suffer persecution." It does not say that only those who want to live above the world will suffer, but those who will live godly "in Christ Jesus." These are the believers who claim that Christ is their all, that they have died with Him and have been crucified with Him, and that they are risen with Him and that they are living in His power. The sad thing is that such persecution often comes from those who are near and dear to us and who ought to know better.

But David is not stopped by such ridicule. He first had to contend with his brother, then with King Saul, and finally with Goliath. He dealt with his brother very quickly answering him as we have seen with questions: "What have I now done? Is there not a cause?" God's reputation was at stake, and that was David's concern.

Is There Not a Cause?

Is there not a cause today for us to stand up and be firm in the faith of the Lord Jesus Christ? This is not a matter of going out and fighting with men or of attacking personalities. It is a matter of getting into the midst of the spiritual battle with the Lord so that those who ridicule and defy Him will no longer go unchallenged. God was defamed and belittled in David's day, but is He not also being defamed and belittled in our time?

When God's Word goes begging these days, is there not a cause? When faith missions have to go out pleading for support, and yet, cannot even send seasoned missionaries back to the field because God's people are not listening to God, is there not a cause? What is the response of some to the plight in which God's work finds itself these days? Do they not peddle shameful untruths about such faith works, slander their leaders, and misrepresent what is being accomplished? But God will not be mocked. Whatsoever a man soweth, that shall he also reap. If we, like Eliab in his day or some in our own day, peddle slander, we will some day be brought face to face with it.

Christian America cannot escape the fact that we are not fulfilling our position in the world by total evangelism today. This is the last strong Protestant nation with the money and the facilities and the personnel to evangelize the world in our time. We have the Bible colleges and Bible institutes and radio programs and young people waiting and ready to go to the field. Yet most of these organizations face a constant struggle to keep their heads above water, and many young people wait in vain for needed support. We cannot pass off our responsibility to these by resorting to slander as Eliab did with regard to David.

There is a great cry in the world today for freedom. The politicians constantly speak of it. Freedom is part of the Christian message but not all agree as to what that freedom should be. Do we want to preserve our freedoms here in North America in order that we might continue to live in plenty and at ease? The Word tells us that whom the Son sets free is free indeed. This is the kind of freedom men need everywhere, and this is the freedom we are commissioned to present to men. We speak of the enslaved nations and of the free world. This distinction is true politically. But the sad fact is that all men are by nature enslaved by sin. The greatest freedom that could come to any man is freedom through Christ.

David could not be stopped by Eliab's criticism and slander. There was a cause and David went right to the heart of it. Israel, God's precious child, was being shamed before hostile nations; and the God of Israel was being defied and blasphemed. This to David was cause enough.

Do we have a cause? In other words, what are we living for? What is our purpose in life? In view of the imminent return of the Lord, this passage from Malachi 3 in the Berkeley version is a stirring reminder to us concerning our responsibilities: "Behold, I send my messenger, and he shall prepare the way before Me, and the Lord whom you seek, will suddenly come to His temple, and the Messenger of the Covenant, in whom you delight, look, He is coming, says the Lord of hosts. But who can endure the day of His coming, and who will be able to stand when He appears? For he is like a refiner's fire and like fullers' soap. He will sit as a refiner and purifier of silver; he will purify the sons of Levi and refine them like gold and silver, so they will present offerings in righteousness to the Lord. . . .

"For I the Lord do not change; return to me and I will return to you . . . 'how shall we return?'

"Then those who revered the Lord conversed with one another; and the Lord listened and heard, and a memorandum book was written before Him, for those who revered the Lord and thought on His name. And they shall be Mine, says the

Lord of hosts in the day on which I prepare My special possession; and I will spare them as a man spares his son who serves him. Then you shall once more distinguish between the righteous and the wicked, between one who serves God and one who does not serve Him."

God does not overlook what we do or fail to do. He will reward those worthy of it and call to account those who have not been faithful to their trust.

We all have a cause that we follow, but is it always the right one? Some in Christian work are always fighting some thing or some one, and one wonders if such are keeping the basic purpose of preaching in view. A Christian worker said to me once, "If you want to get a crowd to listen to you, you must have some prominent issue." This particular man chose to make Communism his issue. But one of the dangers in such things is that a secondary issue is given the place of the primary issue. The primary issue is the preaching of the gospel so that men might be free from the slavery of sin.

David had a cause, and it was a basic one as we have seen. But someone may ask, "Cannot God defend Himself?" Yes, indeed He can! Read the Book of the Revelation and you will see how God enters into history with great judgments in order to bring the inhabitants of the earth in line with His righteous program. But at present, God is dealing in mercy and is seeking men who will stand for His cause. It is hard to grasp and yet it is true that at the present time God is defied by a lack of faith on the part of many believers. The world defies Him, but so do we when we do not trust Him. The world today is not seeing in the lives of the people of God the full demonstration of the power of God provided for those who believe (Eph. 1:19).

This is comparable to the situation in Israel when David was sent to the camp of Saul. David found, as we have seen, the two armies arrayed against each other. The Philistines had come with their man power and weapons, and Israel had organized its army and ranged itself against the Philistines. What a spiritual picture this historical event presents to our minds! Goliath is a type of Satan, so here we have Satan and his armies arrayed against the forces of Jesus Christ. This is an up-to-date picture, for the organized church is facing a hostile world, not in the power of the living God but with methods and programs of man's devising.

David came to the army of Saul to show that it takes more than methods and equipment to win. It takes a man who will dare to believe God. David came to reveal God to Israel as the God who still fights His people's battles.

David and Saul

Apparently David's questions and statements became the talk of the camp, and word was brought to Saul who called David before him. While there David said to his king: "Let not your heart faint, because I will go and fight this man." The humility of David is outstanding here when we consider that he was to replace Saul. He called himself Saul's servant. The reason is that David was first of all God's servant, and he would not raise his hand against one who had been anointed king. David took this position before Saul as an obedient subject to his king, and showed only the highest respect to this man whom he knew he would succeed in the kingship. This attitude on the part of David was well expressed by Paul in Romans 12:3 where he wrote to us to have no unjustifiable notions of our own importance but always to have a sober evaluation of what we are and who we are. This was David's attitude who knew right well that God had a time, a future time, for him to step into the leadership of his nation.

Saul's rejoinder was that David was not able to go against the Philistine to fight with them. Saul said, "Thou art but a youth, and he is a man of war from his youth." Here was a man who was of gigantic stature and had been trained for war from his adolescent years. In this way, Saul sought to discourage David just as Eliab had tried to discourage him with criticism and slander. But David knew his God and would not be put off. It was many centuries later before Paul would put in words the truth that God does not choose the great things of this world to do His work, but calls on those things which the world considers as nothing, to confound the world's wisdom (I Cor. 1:26-29). Herein lies a basic difference between human reasoning and the reasoning of God. David knew his God, and had already seen the hand of God upon his own life in a remarkable way.

David said to Saul, "Thy servant kept his father's sheep, and there came a lion, and a bear, and took a lamb out of the flock: And I went out after him, and smote him, and delivered it out of his mouth: and when he arose against me, I caught him by his beard, and smote him, and slew him." Here was no ordinary courage and no ordinary strength. These were not isolated incidents, for the original indicates that this deliverance from wild animals took place on several occasions.

David's way of approach to such foes and such difficulties was simply this, "I went out against him." Again we find a parallel in the writings of the New Testament: "For though we walk in the flesh, we do not war after the flesh: (For the weapons of our warfare are not carnal, but mighty through God to the pulling down of strong holds;) Casting down imaginations, and every high thing that exalteth itself against the knowledge of God, and bringing into captivity every thought to the obedience of Christ" (II Cor. 10:3-5). David knew about the secret weapons of God. There are spiritual weapons so mighty that nothing of human or even satanic devising can stand against them. Everything can be brought into subjection to God, including our thought life. No wonder that the admonition is, "Be strong in the Lord, and in the power of his might" (Eph. 6:10).

We are told that "the eyes of the Lord run to and fro throughout the whole earth, to show himself strong in the behalf of them whose heart is perfect toward him" (II Chron. 16:9). The word perfect in this connection means a heart set on God with one single purpose. This was the kind of heart that David had, and living as he did in faith in the power of the living God, he had no fear as to the outcome of his fight with Goliath. In II Samuel 17:36,37 we read: "Thy servant slew both the lion and the bear: and this uncircumcised Philistine shall be as one of them, seeing he hath defied the armies of the living God." David continued: "Moreover, The Lord that delivered me out of the paw of the lion, and out of the paw of the bear, he will deliver me out of the hand of this Philistine." Saul was convinced and said to David, "Go, and the Lord be with thee." All David wanted was to be allowed to go meet this "uncircumcised Philistine" meaning this was a man who before God was unclean spiritually, antagonistic to the will and purposes of God, a man who was bringing reproach on God's people and on God's name.

All of us face lions and bears and Goliaths who set at defiance the living God and scorn His people. But where is the Lord God of Elijah? He is still the same today, and those of us who put our trust in Him will find He is not dead. He is the God of the living, and when we face the enemy in the name of this God, we conquer. David looked to God to deliver him. Satan is already a defeated foe. With the mighty weapons that God provides we can stand against Satan. When we resist him, he will flee from us. Let us face all our problems in the strength that God provides.

David had been trained in a school that Goliath knew nothing of, and it was a school Saul had sadly neglected. David was trained in God's school where the preparation is the preparation of the heart through the Word and through personal communion with the Lord. David's public victories were the result of his private and secret fellowship with God. The 91st Psalm tells us: "He that dwelleth in the secret place of the most High shall abide under the shadow of the Almighty." From this we know that if in secret we are right with God and walk with Him, we will find that in the exercise of our faith we will have real victory. Because of this knowledge David could say, "For in the time of trouble he shall hide me in his pavilion: in the secret of his tabernacle shall he hide me; he shall set me up upon a rock" (Ps. 27:5).

David knew as a result of these secret meetings with God that there are weapons which are not carnal but spiritual. These spiritual weapons are greater than anything that man has ever invented. He learned the truth that is laid down in principle in II Corinthians 10:3-5 where we are told that though we walk in the flesh, we do not war after the flesh. Basically, our warfare is a spiritual one. When we win in that area, we will not fail in the other. Nothing can stop a man who will dare to walk in secret with the Lord and strengthen himself in Him. God's work and God's purposes will be done through him.

Our warfare is not "against flesh and blood, but against principalities, against powers, against the rulers of the darkness of this world, against spiritual wickedness in high places, wherefore take unto you the whole armour of God, that ye may be able to withstand in the evil day, and having done all, to stand" (Eph. 6:12,13). This is how David conquered the foe. He met God in private, and thereby conquered the foe in private. As a result he defeated the foe in public. Too many of God's people fight against men rather than the Evil One who is behind the scenes. David knew the secret of spiritual victory, and having found that he moved out in the Name of the Lord.

Saul could not think of a man going into battle without armor, so he put his own armor on David. There was a helmet of brass for his head, a coat of mail to cover his body, and a sword for a weapon. But David refused to go out in armor that he had not tested beforehand.

This does not mean that God could not have used that armor had David worn it, but David would use only the strategy and methods he had proved with God. We all make Saul's mistake in this at times and are not always as aware as was David that it is a mistake. Man-made weapons may have their place in the spiritual warfare because God does use means, but we must be sure they are means that He approves of.

David Meets Goliath

In this fight with Goliath, God supplied David with five smooth stones. He only needed one, but God supplied in abundance. Saul would not go against Goliath even though Saul had a warrior's armor to wear. David refused to wear that armor considering going forth in the name of the Lord to be his real protection. Saul was a coward but David was courageous with a courage from God and not from foolhardiness.

The application to us, of course, is that it is the battle of the Lord against Satan. Goliath, we have noted, is a picture of Satan. Peter tells us that Satan is going about as a roaring lion seeking whom he may devour, but we are to resist him stedfast in the faith. This is the only way we can win. We must put on the whole armor of God and stand in His strength (I Pet. 5:8).

David did not have the appearance of a warrior as he picked five smooth stones out of the brook and with his staff in his hand approached the Philistine. Methods and equipment are secondary, however, when our faith is in the promises of Almighty God. God will use whatever is at hand and whatever we may be able to use as long as we are willing to be used. Faith always ventures forth. The victory is already won the moment we believe God.

David went out and faced the enemy, which was a new experience for Goliath at this time, because ordinarily when he came roaring his defiance, "all the men of Israel, when they saw the man, fled from him, and were sore afraid" (I Sam. 17:24). But David learned the truth of which Paul wrote later when in Philippians 4:13 he said, "I can do all things through Christ which strengtheneth me." There is nothing that can stop us when we have our faith in the right person. John tells us in his first epistle: "For whatsoever is born of God overcometh the world: and this is the victory that overcometh the world, even our faith" (I John 5:4).

Remember that David had first been taunted by his brother when he had dared to venture forth in faith. This is very typical of what we find today for it is often the brother in faith who will try to hold back the one venturing forth in faith. Then Saul sought to discourage David, and this is often the way in Christian circles, where the powers that be, the "bigwigs," discourage any who venture forth in simple faith.

Finally, David is faced with the scorn of Goliath himself. The record is, "And the Philistine came on and drew near unto David; and the man that bare the shield went before him. And when the Philistine looked about, and saw David, he disdained him: for he was but a youth, and ruddy, and of a fair countenance. And the Philistine said unto David, Am I a dog, that thou comest to me with staves? And the Philistine cursed David by his gods. And the Philistine said to David, Come to me, and I will give thy flesh unto the fowl of the air, and to the beasts of the field." This loud boasting might have brought fear to an ordinary heart, especially if one's own family had first brought discouragement and then the "powers that be" had spoken against the venture. But David was not a person of ordinary faith. Neither could Goliath see that this one whom he was so incensed against was more than a stripling, he was the messenger of the living God. Faith is not something that is worn outwardly. It is seen only in its boldness in action.

There was the case of the servant of Elisha who found early one morning that the city in which he and Elisha dwelt was surrounded by the enemy. This man knew these foes were seeking Elisha's life. In great agitation he came before the prophet and told him of the imminent threat. But his master said to him, "Fear not, for they that be with us are more than they that be with them." Then Elisha prayed and said, "Lord, I pray thee, open his eyes that he may see" (II Kings 6:17). The Lord did as the prophet asked. The young man looked and saw the mountains full of horses and chariots of fire round about Elisha. This then is the picture for us to grasp. He who dwells within us is greater than any power that is outside us.

David had godly boldness which was in direct contrast to the proud boasting of Goliath. The tendency today in strongly organized church groups who have neglected the power of the Lord is to lay out the plans of what they think they can do and what they think cannot be done. Then what they do is done in their own strength, and they discourage any others from venturing forth in faith. If we turn to the third chapter of the Book of the Revelation we will see what God thinks of the church of the last days. There He says, "Because thou sayest, I am rich, and increased with goods, and have need of nothing; and knowest not that thou art wretched, and miserable, and poor, and blind, and naked: I counsel thee to buy of me gold tried in the fire, that thou mayest be rich; and white raiment, that thou mayest be clothed, and that the shame of thy nakedness do not appear; and anoint thine eyes with eyesalve, that thou mayest see."

We need to have our eyes opened by the Lord to know the realities of life. Satan is a great boaster and has been from the very beginning when he said, "I will ascend into heaven, I will exalt my throne above the stars of God: I will sit also upon the mount of the congregation, in the sides of the north: I will ascend above the heights of the clouds; I will be like the most High [God]" (Isa. 14:13,14). This characteristic of the Devil is seen in those who are opposed to the Lord.

All such boasting is vain. We learn in Revelation 12:11: "They overcame him [Satan] by the blood of the Lamb, and by the word of their testimony; and they loved not their lives unto the death." God always gives His people the means of overcoming the enemy. When the Christian is clothed in Christ, Satan goes down to defeat.

The Battle Is the Lord's

Faced with Goliath's scorn, David replied: "Thou comest to me with a sword, and with a spear and with a shield: but I come to thee in the name of the Lord of hosts, the God of the armies of Israel, whom thou hast defied. This day will the

Lord deliver thee into mine hand; and I will smite thee, and take thine head from thee; and I will give the carcases of the host of the Philistines this day unto the fowls of the air, and to the wild beasts of the earth; that all the earth may know that there is a God in Israel. And all this assembly shall know that the Lord saveth not with sword and spear: for the battle is the Lord's, and he will give you into our hands" (I Sam. 17:45-47).

What a statement of faith this is! Here is holy boldness, a young man approaching without armor a seasoned warrior who was prepared for battle. No wonder the Psalms have been of such spiritual encouragement to God's people down through the years. David was inspired of God to write much out of his own personal experience so that he could say: "Delight thyself also in the Lord; and he shall give thee the desires of thine heart. Commit thy way unto the Lord; trust also in him; and he shall bring it to pass" (Ps. 37:4,5).

This is the attitude of the heart completely committed to the Lord. This is the kind of heart that God is looking for. He shows himself strong in behalf of those "whose heart is perfect toward him." To those whose one aim and purpose in life is the glory of God and who delight in Him, God gives the desires of their hearts.

It is very possible that the next words from Psalm 37 were written after this experience with Goliath was long past. Here is what David wrote. "The wicked watcheth the righteous, and seeketh to slay him. The Lord will not leave him in his hand, nor condemn him when he is judged. Wait on the Lord, and keep his way, and he shall exalt thee to inherit the land: when the wicked are cut off, thou shalt see it. I have seen the wicked in great power, and spreading himself like a green bay tree. Yet he passed away, and, lo, he was not: yea, I sought him, but he could not be found. Mark the perfect man [that is the mature man, the man who believes and follows God with singleness of heart], and behold the upright: for the end of that man is peace."

When David fought Goliath he was fighting as the representative of Israel just as Goliath was the representative of the Philistine army. The agreement was that if David killed Goliath, the Philistines would be the servants of the Israelites. But if Goliath won, the Israelites would serve the Philistines.

Spiritual Victories Help Others

In David we see not only the picture of a victorious believer, but we have a picture of Christ himself who overcame Satan at Calvary. And just as Christ's victory was not one that affected only Himself but was provided for all who would place their trust in Him, so David's victory over Goliath was not for himself alone but for Israel. When Christ died, He destroyed him that had the power of death, that is the Devil, and delivered those who all their lifetime had been subject to bondage (Heb. 2:14,15). So Christ's death was not for Himself alone. There were others involved.

Apply this to ourselves for a moment. The victory we have today over the enemy reaches farther than just our own hearts and experience. For instance, with regards to salvation there is this additional promise to a person with a family, "Believe on the Lord Jesus Christ and thou shalt be saved, and thy house." Such can pray definitely for the members of their family and look to God to bring each one to a saving knowledge of Christ. Concerning the daily walk, Joshua said, "Choose you this day whom you will serve. As for me and my house, we shall serve the Lord."

David was strengthened for this battle with Goliath through experience. He had trusted God when faced with lions and bears and had been victorious. In each case, he had cast himself on God, and God had sustained him. Now he enters this battle trusting in the integrity of God and His promises.

Such faith comes from meditating on God's Word and applying to the heart the promises that are there for us. God promised Joshua, "Every place that the sole of your foot shall tread upon, that have I given unto you." Joshua found this true, for wherever the Israelites went trusting in the Lord, the land was given into their hands. It was God who gave it to them and God who promised, "I will be with thee: I will not fail thee, nor forsake thee. Be strong and of a good courage . . . that thou mayest prosper whithersoever thou goest." Again the promise was given, "Be strong and of good courage; be not afraid, neither be thou dismayed: for the Lord thy God is with thee." David knew these promises and encouraged himself in secret before the Lord.

In the 18th Psalm which is also found in II Samuel 22 David rehearses what God has done. In its form in II Samuel, the Psalm reads: "As for God, his way is perfect; the word of the Lord is tried: he is a buckler to all them that trust in him. For who is God, save the Lord? and who is a rock, save our God? God is my strength and power: and he maketh my way perfect. He maketh my feet like hinds' feet: and setteth me upon my high places. He teacheth my hands to war; so that a bow of steel is broken by mine arms. Thou hast also given me the shield of thy salvation: and thy gentleness hath made me great. Thou hast enlarged my steps under me; so that my feet did not slip. I have pursued mine enemies, and destroyed them; and turned not again until I had consumed them. And I have consumed them, and wounded them, that they could not arise: yea, they are fallen under my feet. For thou hast girded me with strength unto the battle: them that rose up against me hast thou subdued under me. Thou hast also given me the necks of mine enemies, that I might destroy them that hate me."

It is with such confidence and promises that David was the conqueror of Goliath. David was sustained and strengthened by the Word of God. On the other hand, Israel was helpless because it was fighting under a leader who had forfeited the anointing power of God, by his disobedience.

We have the same situation today with regard to organized Christendom. Wherever the anointing of the Holy Spirit has been forfeited, the church is weak and helpless. But where men and women accept God's Word and are controlled by His Spirit, they find they have the authority to win the fight against the forces of evil. There is nothing that can stop a man or a church that is following in the way of the Lord, because we read in Ephesians 1:19: "And what is the exceeding greatness of his power to us-ward who believe, according to the working of his mighty power, Which he wrought in Christ, when he raised him from the dead." Further on in the same letter we read that God has raised us up together to sit with Christ in heavenly places. We fight battles whose victories are assured.

So far as David was concerned the victory against Goliath was already won. All David had to do was to commit himself to God and allow the Lord to work through him. Remember, we have the victory that overcomes the world also, even our faith.

David, we also find, refused to imitate the enemies methods by wearing Saul's armor. "Put on the armor," the king said, "and put on the sword, put on this helmet, and this coat of mail, then you will be able to go out and fight Goliath." But David refused this because in so doing he would simply have been imitating the enemy. Today we need to learn this lesson all over again. Somehow or another we seem to feel that in order to do a great job we must imitate the world. Some think the only way to reach young people is to give them what they want. Then by giving Christian names to what these young persons want these leaders think they will reach them for the Lord. But this is folly. The real armor for David and for us is an invisible armor, but an effective one, nevertheless. When we put on this armor which is Christ Jesus himself we go out to victory. Goliath could not see the armor that David wore, and so scoffed at him, calling him a dog. David, on the other hand, knew that he was going in the name of the Lord, and that in his case physical armor was not necessary. His victory was to be won by the might and power of the living God instead of by the usual weapons of warfare.

The desires of the heart are given to the person who delights himself in the Lord. But what does this mean? The answer is found in Isaiah 58:13 which says, "Thou shalt honour him, not doing thine own ways, nor finding thine own pleasure, nor speaking thine own words: Then shalt thou delight thyself in the Lord." There are four things included here, and the best example of a life lived according to these four standards is that of the Lord Jesus himself. In His High Priestly prayer in John 17 our Saviour said, "I have glorified thee on the earth: I have finished the work which thou gavest me to do. And now, O Father, glorify thou me with thine own self with the glory which I had with thee before the world was." All through this chapter the Lord Jesus enumerates the things He did with the one purpose of glorifying His Father in heaven.

We might well ask ourselves if this is our goal and service. I heard a servant of God say one day, and I repeat it here for our serious consideration: "I would rather go through the great Tribulation with all its horrors, than to stand at the Judgment Seat of Christ where many Christians will be judged for the poor quality of their works and service." He said this because so many Christians today pay little attention to the honor of God.

Victorious Faith

The kind of faith David exhibited is clearly defined for us in Mark 11:22: "Have faith in God. For verily I say unto you, That whosoever shall say unto this mountain, Be thou removed, and be thou cast into the sea; and shall not doubt in his heart, but shall believe that those things which he saith shall come to pass; he shall have whatsoever he saith." When David went against Goliath he did not say, "I am praying that God will give you into mine hands." He declared definitely and finally that God would give Goliath into his hands. David went before Goliath with the note of victory on his lips.

How could David be sure of this? He had only one motive and purpose in fighting Goliath and that was to uphold the honor of God. In the second place, David had implicit faith in God and was confident that God would not let him down.

It was because of acting on the basis of such faith that

victory was given David. "And it came to pass, when the Philistine arose, and came and drew nigh to meet David, that David hastened, and ran toward the army to meet the Philistine. And David put his hand in his bag, and took thence a stone, and slang it, and smote the Philistine in his forehead, that the stone sunk into his forehead; and he fell upon his face to the earth. So David prevailed over the Philistine with a sling and with a stone, and smote the Philistine, and slew him; but there was no sword in the hand of David. Therefore David ran, and stood upon the Philistine, and took his sword, and drew it out of the sheath thereof, and slew him, and cut off his head therewith. And when the Philistines saw their champion was dead, they fled."

So then, faith wrought the victory. When faith is in the right person there will always be victory. But faith that is true faith has to be appropriated and put in action, otherwise, it is not faith at all. For us to say we believe, and yet not act, is faithlessness and mockery. James makes this very plain in his letter: "What doth it profit, my brethren, though a man say he hath faith, and have not works? can [that] faith save him?" This is an exact translation of this passage. It means that faith that does not produce works is not faith. "Faith, if it hath not works, is dead, being alone," James adds. He continues: "For as the body without the spirit is dead, so faith without works is dead." There is a great deal of talk these days about faith, but true faith is active and moves forward.

David's response to faith was simple. There was first of all the secret of his confidence stated when he said that he came to Goliath in the name of the Lord and of the armies of Israel. The source of his strength was the same God, and the certainty of his victory was the same Lord of Glory.

One thing we must seek in every contest is to have complete victory, not a partial one. David used the stone on Goliath and the giant fell to the ground. But David did more. He made sure that victory was complete. He took Goliath's sword and smote off his head.

There is a parallel in the spiritual realm. We must learn

what it is to put sin and our spiritual foe, Satan, under our feet. In Ephesians 1:22 it is said of Christ that God "put all things under his feet." This is illustrated for us in the 10th chapter of Joshua where we find the kings that opposed Israel were brought before Joshua. He said to the leaders of his army: "Come near, put your feet upon the necks of these kings. And they came near, and put their feet upon the necks of them." Following that, Joshua smote those kings and slew them. Victory has been made possible to us. Now we must see it through to the finish.

God's own program for the ages calls for the complete subjugation of all enemies. "Then cometh the end, when he shall have delivered up the kingdom to God, even the Father; when he shall have put down all rule and all authority and power. For he must reign, till he hath put all enemies under his feet. The last enemy that shall be destroyed is death. For he hath put all things under his feet" (I Cor. 15:24).

On the death of Goliath, the Philistine army began to run in terror, and the people of Israel followed after them to take the spoils. This is always true. Wherever the faithful servant or servants of God carry through some project of victory, the unbelieving and faithless crowd will always come in seeking what it considers its share.

That same crowd may have through envy and jealousy held back the victory for a time, but as soon as the victory is won, they want to climb on the bandwagon.

May God give us grace to believe Him and through faith not to be defeated Christians but victorious children of the living God. May God stir our hearts so that we will not be ashamed of Jesus Christ our Lord.

CHAPTER THREE

THE PRICE OF POPULARITY

I Samuel 18

With the slaying of Goliath, David's life entered into an entirely new phase. Up to this point, even though he had had access to the court of Saul, he had also been going home between times to tend his father's sheep. We learn, however, that Saul "took him that day, and would let him go no more home to his father's house" (I Sam. 18:2). The king saw that he had found a valuable man. Though the Spirit of God had departed from Saul He had come upon David, and Saul was not blind to the contribution such a Spirit-directed person could make to the kingdom of Israel.

Spiritually speaking, the two men were opposites. David was controlled by the Holy Spirit whereas Saul was a carnal-minded man. It was not long before Saul's selfishness and jealousy destroyed his better judgment with regard to David.

Jonathan, Saul's eldest son, loved and admired David so much that the Scripture says, "The soul of Jonathan was knit with the soul of David" (v. 1). Jonathan demonstrated this love and devotion by stripping himself of his robe and his garments, his sword, his bow, and his girdle also, giving them all to David. This was new equipment for Israel's future king, for his battle against Goliath had been won with a sling and a stone and finally the giant's own sword. Undoubtedly, this gesture on Jonathan's part pleased David, for he now had the equipment of the king's own son, yet it did not make David haughty or proud. He stayed the same humble young man as he was when tending his father's sheep.

David knew he had been anointed to the kingship, but at this point Saul did not know it which, of course, was just as well for David's safety. He went wherever Saul sent him and "behaved himself wisely: and Saul set him over the men of war, and he was accepted in the sight of all the people, and also in the sight of Saul's servants" (v. 5). David was submissive without any show of arrogance whatsoever. He very likely was a member of Saul's bodyguard which shows the high esteem in which Saul held him. At the same time it demonstrates that David had no personal ambition with regard to the throne. He was in a position to do harm to Saul, but it is apparent from this and other portions of Scripture that such a thought was abhorrent to him.

David became popular with the people. This is clear from the fact that he was accepted in their sight and in the sight of Saul's servants. He had been faithful in taking care of his father's sheep, a task for a servant rather than for a son of the household. But it was in those days that he met God again and again and learned to know Him intimately. To the man who learns to be faithful in little things God gives greater responsibilities. This was true in David's experience but it did not give him an inflated idea of his own importance. It did not "go to his head" as we would say.

Another test faced David, one that resulted from his popularity and ability. "And it came to pass as they came, when David was returned from the slaughter of the Philistine, that the women came out of all cities of Israel, singing and dancing, to meet king Saul, with tabrets, with joy, and with instruments of musick. And the women answered one another as they played, and said, Saul hath slain his thousands, and David his ten thousands" (vv. 6,7).

One must be careful of praise because of the ease with which the carnal element can enter into it. These women came out praising the man, but their very praise became a test for David. God permitted this and David came through victorious: "David behaved himself wisely in all his ways; and the Lord was with him" (v. 14).

Saul's reaction on the other hand was what one would expect from a carnal man. The king had taken David into his own household, but the moment the servant received more praise than the king, Saul lost his temper. We read, "And Saul was very wroth, and the saying displeased him; and he said, They have ascribed unto David ten thousands, and to me they have ascribed but thousands: and what can he have more but the kingdom?" (v. 8). It would seem from this that Saul began to suspect that David was the man who had been chosen to replace him.

In all this God was preparing David to be a good ruler. These experiences also showed the carnality of Saul who was rejected because he rejected God.

Saul eyed David from that day forward, and his anger turned to fear when he saw how wisely David behaved himself. When Saul saw that the honor and praise that he thought should have been his was going to David, his carnal nature took over and from then on he cast an envious eye at David.

The carnal man will often try to cover up his carnality by an outward show of religion. Saul, we are told, prophesied in the midst of the house (v. 10), but this gift had its source in the evil spirit that came upon him. His prophesying was not the work of the Holy Spirit but of a fallen spirit. Demons can enable certain persons to imitate miraculous gifts. Moses found this out when he went before Pharaoh to seek the liberation of the Children of Israel. Pharaoh's magicians performed miracles also though only up to a certain point. Evil spirits, however, cannot produce spiritual life.

David, as at other times when the evil spirit came upon Saul, played with a harp in order to sooth the King's troubled mind. But Saul refused help. He had a javelin in his hand and cast it at David saying, "I will smite David even to the wall with it. And David avoided out of his presence twice" (v. 11). David though chosen of God was in constant danger of his life. Would God be able to take care of him? Yes, for He is the God who changes not (Mal. 3:6). This is our assurance also: "Being confident of this very thing, that he which hath begun a good work in you will perform it until the day of Jesus Christ" (Phil. 1:6). No man can withstand God. When God chooses to do something, He will see it through regardless of the opposition against Him.

David chose the way that saved his life. Many years later a greater than David was to say, "If any man will come after me, let him deny himself, and take up his cross daily, and follow me. For whosoever will save his life shall lose it: but whosoever will lose his life for my sake, the same shall save it" (Luke 9:23,24). David did not retaliate. He had learned the ways of war, and it would have only been human nature to have wanted to grab that javelin and throw it back at Saul. David might have excused such an action by reason of the fact that God had chosen him to be king. But he had chosen God's way of life. He avoided the javelin and did not seek revenge.

Saul was not through with David, however. Saul's fear of David increased as his envy of David increased. He demoted David, making him head of a thousand men, a much lesser position than he had held in the household of the king.

Furthermore, as leader of a thousand men, David was put in a very dangerous position in time of battle. Here again David behaved himself wisely and the Lord was with him. He went out and came in before the people but not before Saul who refused to have him any longer in his presence.

Like Paul at a later date, David learned in whatsoever state he found himself to be content. Here are Paul's exact words in Philippians 4:11-13: "Not that I speak in respect of want: for I have learned, in whatsoever state I am, therewith to be content. I know both how to be abased, and I know how to abound: every where and in all things I am instructed both to be full and to be hungry, both to abound and to suffer need. I can do all things through Christ which strengtheneth me."

David let the Holy Spirit lead and direct him so that he was able to cope with every situation as it came up. He did not fight for his rights as God's anointed king but left the time and situation in the hands of God. Though demoted and put in a place of extreme danger, he was faithful to his responsibility and to his God.

Can we be trusted to be faithful when the lesser tasks or the dangerous tasks are given us? Let us find God's place and fill it, controlled at all times by the Holy Spirit. Then we will be blessed as was David.

Popularity has its attractive side, but it carries with it spiritual dangers. There is always a price to pay for it, and sometimes it comes high. Some can take popularity and not be hurt by it, others cannot. Pride arising in the human heart for any reason is not good. Then there are always those who become jealous of anyone who seems to be well liked by others. Perhaps these dangers, internal and external, help keep a person on the alert. The Lord knows how much any of us can take of these things and always provides a way of escape. This is His promise: "There hath no temptation taken you but such as is common to man: but God is faithful, who will not suffer you to be tempted above that ye are able; but will with the temptation also make a way to escape" (I Cor. 10:13). David was tested, but he was never left without a way out of the testing.

David knew where his strength lay so that praise only turned him to give God the glory. It did not change his humble attitude toward life. On the other hand Saul's reaction to the praise given David changed Saul for the worse.

David waited eight years before he became king of Judah and these were years of deep testing. It was during this time that he wrote many of the Psalms. He was often in hiding and almost constantly in danger of his life. These were years when God was training his man to be Israel's shepherd.

God tests His servants and perfects them. We can see this in the life of Moses who for 40 years remained hidden away in a desert area as God prepared him for the task of delivering Israel. Moses thought he was ready when he was 40 years of age, but he still needed 40 more years of training under the private hand of the Divine Teacher. Finally, Moses became the instrument God could use. David spent eight years of training through severe trials of various kinds before he was ready for the position to which God had appointed him.

Let us not become discouraged if after we surrender our lives to God He permits testings and trials to come. They will always come. Young people write to me or speak to me in services about this. One of their greatest questions is why things are so adverse after they have given themselves completely to the Lord. We know first from the Scriptures and then from experience that testings are essential for our spiritual training. They are needed before God can trust us with the responsibilities of spiritual leadership.

David was tested by popularity on the one hand, and jealousy on the other to see whether he would keep on trusting God. He stood the test, though it is right here that many of God's servants have fallen. Too many of us want what we consider our rights or the praise we think we should receive. We fail to realize how much we are hurting our own lives in doing this. It may be for our own good that God allows someone else to receive the glory and the honor that we feel should be ours.

In the case of David, God let men pile praise on him because he knew David's heart. The testings David faced in his own home showed that there was true humility of character about him. He was the eighth son and was hardly considered a real member of the family at all. When Samuel went to Jesse's home to anoint one of his sons and make a feast, David was left out by his father and brothers. He was treated more as a servant than a son. But he did not complain, he just kept on enjoying fellowship with God.

David's popularity did not arise until after his defeat of Goliath. Then opposition from Saul arose. He hated and feared David and attempted to bring about his death. The king was crafty, however. He planned David's death but not in such an obvious way that he, Saul, could be charged with it.

He had promised that he would give his daughter in marriage to the man who defeated Goliath. This was not done right away. Saul plotted to use this promise, however, as a means of getting rid of his rival. He said to David: "Behold my elder daughter Merab, her will I give thee to wife: only be thou valiant for me, and fight the Lord's battles. For Saul said, Let not mine hand be upon him, but let the hand of the Philistines be upon him" (v. 17). David was still his humble self, and replied to Saul: "Who am I? and what is my life, or my father's family in Israel, that I should be son in law to the king?" (v. 18).

Saul was not a man of his word. He gave Merab in marriage to Adriel the Meholathite (v. 19). No doubt Saul tried in this way to stir up David's resentment and cause him to say or do something Saul could use as an excuse for killing him. But this failed. David showed no resentment though he must have felt the insult offered him.

Then Saul learned that his younger daughter, Michal, loved David. This delighted the scheming king for it provided him with the opportunity for adding another condition to the marriage, a condition which Saul hoped would rid him of his prospective son-in-law. Michal was promised to David in the hope that she would be "a snare to him, and that the hand of the Philistines may be against him" (v. 21).

David had no dowry to offer, especially for the hand of a king's daughter, but Saul waved all of that aside. He said that it would be dowry enough for David to go out and kill 100 Philistines and bring their foreskins to Saul as proof that they had been killed. The Philistines did not practice circumcision but the Israelites did. It was a mark of their separation from the nations around them. The Philistines, on the other hand, looked on the practice with abhorrence. It is very clear from this strategy that Saul hoped David would be so hated by the Philistines that they would hunt him down and destroy him. Thus, David would die at the hand of a Gentile nation and Saul's hands would be clean, at least in the eyes of the Israelites.

David knew that in order to be useful to God he must die to self and arise in the strength of God. The seed of grain must die before it can multiply. David behaved himself well before men and God, and went out and slew not 100 but 200 Philistines and brought Saul the proof. This made Saul more apprehensive than ever, and his mind was made more uneasy than before. Saul was not sure, but the more he saw of this remarkable young man the more he was convinced that David was to be Israel's next king.

Here was a young man who had killed Goliath and yet had remained humble and exemplary in his conduct. He was exceedingly popular with the people. None of Saul's plans to destroy David prospered. They were all brought to nothing. It became increasingly evident to Saul that the Lord had departed from him but was with David.

David knew the truth of Psalm 37:5: "Commit thy way unto the Lord; trust also in him; and he shall bring it to pass." This Psalm grew out of his own experience. Here you find no self-seeking. He was not a time server but a man who stood humble before his God, seeking to please Him only. David served in the spirit of Philippians 2:3 which reads: "Let nothing be done through strife or vainglory; but in lowliness of mind let each esteem other better than themselves. Look not every man on his own things, but every man also on the things of others. Let this mind be in you, which was also in Christ Jesus." There are altogether too few people like that today. Even Paul in his time found it difficult to find men who would fully follow the Lord. Concerning Timothy, however, Paul could say in Philippians 2:20: "For I have no man likeminded, who will naturally care for your state. For all seek their own, not the things which are Jesus Christ's." Selfishness lies at the root of much spiritual failure in any age.

Is it any wonder James wrote: "But he giveth more grace. Wherefore he saith, God resisteth the proud, but giveth grace unto the humble. Submit yourselves therefore to God. Resist the devil, and he will flee from you" (James 4:6). Such humility comes only through the grace of God. The best place to learn it is at the feet of Jesus not only in prayer but through the Word and through the operation of His Spirit. Our Lord said in the days of His ministry: "Come unto me, all ye that labour and are heavy laden, and I will give you rest. Take my yoke upon you, and learn of me; for I am meek and lowly in heart: and ye shall find rest unto your souls" (Matt. 11:28,29). A yoke is a harness that binds two together in the same common task. If the task God gives us seems to be menial, let us remember that our yokefellow is the Lord of Glory.

It is well then that Paul should write to us not to think of ourselves more highly than we ought to think, but to think soberly (Rom. 12:3).

Another very plain passage is Hebrews 13:12: "Wherefore Jesus also, that he might sanctify the people with his own blood, suffered without the gate." What does the writer mean by these words? He means that Christ was considered to be a criminal and as such was not allowed to die inside Jerusalem but must die outside the gates. And so the application is made to us: "Let us go forth therefore unto him without the camp, bearing his reproach. For here have we no continuing city, but we seek one to come" (vv. 13,14). This was the attitude David had toward the things of life. His whole heart was given over to following his Lord wherever He directed.

It was no wonder, then, that all of Saul's plans for David's death fell through. God made the wrath of man to praise him, and the rest He restrained (Ps. 76:10). When David returned safely from the slaughter of the Philistines, Saul could not take it and decided to cast off all pretense with regard to seeking David's death.

He did not work underhandedly any longer. He came out into the open and told his servants and his son Jonathan that they should kill David. There was no other path open to David but flight, and this becomes the subject of our next chapter.

Is Your All on the Altar?

You have longed for sweet peace, and for faith to increase,
  And have earnestly, fervently prayed;
But you cannot have rest, or be perfectly blest
  Until all on the altar is laid.

Oh, we never can know what the Lord will bestow
Of the blessings for which we have prayed,
Till our body and soul He doth fully control,
And our all on the altar is laid.

Is your all on the altar of sacrifice laid?
Your heart, does the Spirit control?
You can only be blest and have peace and sweet rest,
As you yield Him your body and soul.

CHAPTER FOUR

PERSECUTED, FLEEING, BUT NOT FORSAKEN

I Samuel 19 with Psalm 59

Saul's deep-seated jealousy and animosity toward David were no longer covered. The king openly sought David's death and tried to enlist his oldest son Jonathan in this evil enterprise. But Jonathan loved David and interceded for him. This stayed the hand of Saul for a little, but a carnal Christian who is pursuing ends that are at variance with the will of God can be cruel, heartless and dangerous. Men bereft of the Spirit of God have done some terrible deeds.

When David realized he had to flee, he naturally went to his own house. But his home was not a safe place for him. Being human David had his weaknesses, and one of those weaknesses showed itself in some of the women he married. It is doubtful if Michal was a true believer, and his marriage to her was a source of trouble to him.

Saul had David's house surrounded by his soldiers who were instructed to watch all night long and then to kill David when the morning came. David knew, of course, that they were there and so did Michal who, in spite of her lack of spirituality, loved her husband and sought his escape. She let David down from the house through a window, and he made his way safely in the darkness through the ranks of his enemies. But while he was gone, Michal conceived a scheme to give him more time to effect his escape. Seemingly she had no conscience about telling lies if they served her purposes. She took what was apparently a large-sized image and laid it in the bed and put a pillow of goats' hair for the bolster, and covered it with a cloth. This made it appear that someone was lying there sick. When Saul's messengers came to arrest David, she said, "He is sick." This bit of camouflage she had put together was deceptive enough at a distance to pass their examination. But when Saul told them to go back and to bring David on the bed if necessary, they soon found what deception had been practiced on them. Then, when Saul said to his daughter, "Why hast thou deceived me so, and sent away mine enemy, that he is escaped?" her answer was another lie: "He said unto me, Let me go; why should I kill thee?" (I Sam. 19:17). David said no such thing.

Out of this experience he wrote Psalm 59. In it he pours out his heart for deliverance (vv. 1,2), and declares his innocence saying, "Strong men are banding together to attack me, not for my transgression, nor for my sin, O Lord. Without any wrong of mine, they run and prepare themselves" (vv. 3,4, Berkeley). He felt keenly the pressure of the lies and persecution of his enemies.

This is a good Psalm for us to read when we are being pressured by foes or hounded or criticized because of belonging to the Lord. Perhaps our troubles have been financial; but whatever they are, let us learn from David how to triumph in them. He cast himself upon the deliverance of God, and found his Lord providing the way of escape.

In the second place, David prayed himself out of a sense of helplessness into a state of quiet confidence. Following this, he burst into a song of victory. All of this was true even though the enemy still pursued him. He had confidence in God that He would save his soul and also that God was in complete control of all the details of his life. David escaped from panic and entered into a song of triumph at the end of the Psalm, having by God's grace evaded the traps and snares set for his feet.

His description is very vivid as he says concerning his enemies, "They return at evening: they [snarl] make a noise like a dog, and go round about the city. Behold, they belch out with their mouth, swords are in their lips." This was his description of Saul's men as they surrounded David's home, seeking his very life. Yet in it all David was conscious of being in God's hands.

Can we like David commit our way to the Lord, trusting also in Him, and letting Him bring it to pass? (Ps. 37:5). This has been a portion of God's Word that has helped me hundreds of times, and is something we should all know and practice.

David was not overwhelmed by his enemies but in verse 8 of Psalm 59 he said, "But thou, O Lord, shalt laugh at them; thou shalt have all the heathen [Gentiles] in derision." So in this fact David relaxed and rested his case in God, for God was his strength. This is what David says in verse 9: "Because of his strength will I wait upon thee: for God is my defence."

There is a difference between God being our strength and our stronghold or defence and one from whom we derive these things. We are but weak vessels and cannot contain of ourselves much of God's strength for protection. But when like David we can say He is my strength, not merely that He gives me strength, then we find Him in the fullness of His strength. It is better to be able to say that He is our defence than to say that He gives us defence. This is the truth emphasized in Ephesians 6 where we read: "Be strong in the Lord, and in the power of his might . . . put on the whole armour of God, that ye may be able to withstand in the evil day, and having done all, to stand." He is both our strength and our might. We not only need righteousness and peace but we find in I Corinthians 1:30 that Christ is made unto us righteousness and peace. The reason is that Christ lives in us, and this fact makes all the difference in the world.

David emphasizes this same truth in the 18th Psalm where he cried out: "I will love thee, O Lord, my strength. The Lord is my rock, and my fortress, and my deliverer; my God, my strength, in whom I will trust." The fact to grasp is that God does not give us these because He is Himself all these to us. The way of the Lord is perfect and the Word of the Lord has been tried and found true. Just as David found the Lord his buckler, his strong tower and his safety, so the Lord is all of these things to us also.

David cried to the Lord for mercy. This is a word very prominent in the Psalms of David and is found in the 10th verse of Psalm 59. Then in verse 11 he prays not for the killing of his enemies, but for their discipline. He pleads: "Slay them not, lest my people forget: scatter them by thy power; and bring them down, O Lord our shield." He wants God to deal with these enemies in such a way that they will be brought to a proper understanding of the ways of God. David wants some chastisement to fall upon them that will cause their return to the Lord.

In the 16th and 17th verses which are the climax of the Psalm, David said, "But I will sing of thy power; yea, I will sing aloud of thy mercy in the morning: for thou hast been my defence and refuge in the day of my trouble. Unto thee, O my strength, will I sing: for God is my defence, and the God of my mercy." David had learned to sing while surrounded by his enemies. He prayed himself out of panic, out of fear, out of doubt into confidence and joyful song. Faith is the substance of things hoped for, the evidence of things not seen. This David had learned and was praising God even though his own deliverance was not yet in evidence.

David's circumstances had not changed because the enemy still surrounded his house. So great, however, was his confidence in God that his cry for deliverance became a calm waiting upon God even while the enemy pressed him on every side. God was everything to him, all he needed.

All this came about because David waited on the Lord. This we gather from verse 9: "Because of his strength will I wait upon thee: for God is my defence." The same truth is emphasized in Psalm 121 where David said, "I will lift up mine eyes unto the hills, from whence cometh my help. My help cometh from the Lord, which made heaven and earth. He will not suffer thy foot to be moved: he that keepeth thee will not slumber. . . . The Lord shall preserve thy going out and thy coming in from this time forth, and even for evermore." Knowing this David waited on the Lord, something we so often forget to do. We pray but we do not wait. We find ourselves in trouble and we pray, but we do not wait. We ask but by our actions suggest we do not expect an answer.

The promise the Saviour made in Matthew 7:7 is, "Ask, and it shall be given you; seek, and ye shall find; knock, and it shall be opened unto you." We should wait for the answer. There is a time for waiting in the presence of God. This same unfortunate hurry is often seen in our devotional times when in the morning we rush off to the duties of the day without adequate preparation in the presence of the Lord.

David, on the other hand, took time enough to have his fears calmed and the assurance of deliverance come to his soul even while his enemies surrounded his house, waiting to take his life.

David full of faith, full of joy, and full of confidence, is not presumptuous; but when the opportunity to flee was given, he made his escape and went to Samuel. Word was brought to Saul as to David's whereabouts, and Saul sent soldiers to arrest him. When they came near to where Samuel was, the Spirit of God came upon them and they prophesied. They returned to Saul and he sent a second group and they likewise prophesied. The same happened to the third group, and finally Saul himself came and he prophesied. They could not touch David because God was with him and would not turn him over to his enemy. Saul stripped himself of his armor and his outer garments and fell down in what appeared to be a trance. So once again David was saved from the envy and hatred of Saul.

CHAPTER FIVE

A GOOD MAN IN BAD COMPANY

I Samuel 20, 21

The road to victory and the road to defeat are never too far apart. David found sanctuary with Samuel but unfortunately he did not continue in that place of safety. The 20th chapter opens with the words: "And David fled from Naioth in Ramah, and came and said before Jonathan, What have I done? what is mine iniquity? and what is my sin before thy father, that he seeketh my life?" We must remember, of course, that David was not sinlessly perfect. God never glosses over the sins of His servants, not even over this man whom the Scripture describes as a man after God's own heart. Biographers are often biased either for or against the person they write about, and for this reason often end up with a distorted picture of their subject. But not so with God. He shows us the true life of a man. God, of course, sees the heart of a man which man cannot see.

Because of the strain and pressure David was under, Satan was able to enter one of his fiery darts through a chink in David's spiritual armor. He became so depressed for awhile that he felt death was the only alternative and said to Jonathan: "There is but a step between me and death" (v. 3). Doubt had entered David's heart. His faith had begun to lapse for a time, at least.

Once doubt lays hold of the heart, other sins follow in quick order. This is why the Lord admonishes us in Ephesians 6:16 to "take the shield of faith, wherewith ye shall be able to quench the fiery darts of the wicked." Satan will shoot at us from the most unexpected directions and only the shield of faith can quench his evil darts.

It was not long after doubt began to enter David's heart that truth left. He asked Jonathan to sound out Saul with regard to his attitude toward David and then bring him the word. David should have been eating at Saul's table, but if Saul inquired as to David's whereabouts, Jonathan was to cover up for David by saying he had gone to Bethlehem to a special family feast. David had no intention of being in Bethlehem, so this was a lie.

A little later when he fled to Ahimelech, the priest, David again resorted to an untruth. Ahimelech was afraid that David's presence before him was the beginning of trouble, but David sought to quiet the priest's fears by saying, "The king hath commanded me a business, and hath said unto me, Let no man know any thing of the business whereabout I send thee, and what I have commanded thee: and I have appointed my servants to such and such a place" (21:2).

As David's lies increased, so did his fear of Saul increase. "And David arose, and fled that day for fear of Saul, and went to Achish the king of Gath." Goliath whom David had slain had been a subject of the king of Gath, yet David sought protection at the court of this enemy.

Again fear laid hold of David when the servants of Achish spoke against him. "And David laid up these words in his heart, and was sore afraid of Achish the king of Gath" (21:12). David was in bad company. No wonder he lived in fear. Fear is always the enemy of faith. A man grows and triumphs to the extent that his faith overcomes his fear. To believe God and rest in His Word enables the believer to enjoy the promises of God.

This was a sad chapter in David's life but David was not forsaken. God permitted these tests in order to teach David some very valuable lessons. The Lord was preparing him for the throne where he would have to meet much greater tests.

David learned through these experiences that he could always rely on God's faithfulness and love.

A third matter David needed to learn was there was no need to fear what men might do to him. Fear enters into our lives when we begin to doubt God's motives concerning us. The Word of God assures us that all things work together for good to them that love God, to them who are called according to His purpose (Rom. 8:28). But we are not always ready to accept this. Sometimes it takes some hard discipline before we begin to appreciate what God is doing for us.

When our Saviour came walking on the water to the disciples, they thought He was a spirit and cried out in fear. But His word of comfort to them was: "Be of good cheer, it is I." There is nothing to be afraid of when the Lord is around. He has promised never to leave us nor forsake us.

Just before leaving His disciples the Lord Jesus said, "Peace I leave with you, my peace I give unto you: not as the world giveth, give I unto you. Let not your heart be troubled, neither let it be afraid" (John 14:27). In the 16th chapter of John He said, "These things I have spoken unto you, that in me ye might have peace. In the world ye shall have tribulation: but be of good cheer; I have overcome the world" (v. 33).

We learn from this the need of obedience to the Spirit of God. The promise is that the Spirit is given to be with us forever. According to I John 2:27: "The anointing which ye have received of him abideth in you . . . and hath taught you, that ye all abide in him." The second part is what we often forget. We need to abide in Him. Why this is so John also tells us: "And now, little children, abide in him, that, when he shall appear, we may have confidence, and not be ashamed before him at his coming."

David also received the Spirit's anointing, and like us he needed to abide in Him for victory. There was this vital difference, however. In the Old Testament economy, when a man on whom the Holy Spirit came, rebelled, the Spirit might leave him as happened to Saul. This was why David prayed after deeply grieving God: "Take not thy holy spirit from me" (Ps. 51:11).

Today God's Spirit abides with the believer for ever, but disobedience to Him results in loss of fellowship now and loss of rewards when the Lord returns. The need of the believer at any time is to walk in obedience to the Spirit of God.

Faith must be tested. We often have to learn by painful experience and the bitter consequences of our waywardness what follows in our lives when we do not trust the Lord. This was a lesson David had to learn. God included this experience of David's in His Word in order to help us learn better how to live for Him.

David did not know that his lies would bring trouble to Ahimelech. David was hungry and asked for food. While conversing with the priest, he saw Doeg, chief herdsmen for King Saul near the sanctuary. This man was an Edomite, not an Israelite, who wore a cloak of religion to cover up the true condition of his heart. He was a tool of Saul's, cruel and unscrupulous, and it is likely that David's heart skipped a beat when he saw this wicked man.

David had no weapon with which to defend himself, so he asked Ahimelech if there was not some sword to be had. It was then that Ahimelech remembered the sword of Goliath which had been put in the Tabernacle. David gladly received it and then fled to Achish, to the country and people from which Goliath had come.

It was only about a year before this that David had slain the giant. Now he sought safety at the court of Achish and entered with Goliath's sword in his hand. If David had reason to fear for his life in the court of Saul, he had equal reason to fear in the court of Achish. David was reaping what he had sowed in leaving the sanctuary provided by Samuel and letting fear plan his movements.

Had David stayed with Samuel no harm would have come to Ahimelech and his fellow priests; but David's presence among them, of which they were entirely innocent proved to be their death warrant. Doeg did exactly what David feared he would do. He told Saul everything he had seen and undoubtedly added things that were not true. Then Saul called the priests, 86 of them, though one stayed by the stuff, and Saul charged them with aiding David. In his violent rage Saul ordered his servants to kill the priests, and his servants refused. This kind of action, however, was not above Doeg, who not only killed them, but later went to their homes and killed their wives and children. Only one man, Abiathar by name, escaped to tell David the whole sad story.

This was a terrible tragedy for which David took the blame though the crime lay with Saul.

In passing, this observation should be made, though it in no wise excuses Saul. Many years before this event the Lord had instructed Samuel to tell Eli the high priest that his house would be cut off because of their sins. All these priests who were killed at the command of Saul were descendants of Eli. Only Abiathar was left alive. He served David all his life, but after David's death he was removed from the priesthood. This was done by Solomon who said to him, "Get thee to Anathoth, unto thine own fields; for thou art worthy of death: but I will not at this time put thee to death, because thou barest the ark of the Lord before David my father, and because thou hast been afflicted in all wherein my father was afflicted" (I Kings 2:26). Thus the last member of the house of Eli was removed from being a priest to the Lord. This was the final chapter in the fulfillment of Samuel's prophecy.

David's flight had not removed him from danger, and it only served to bring trouble to others. Though Achish, the king of Gath, received him, David found himself among enemies. The servants of Achish said to their king, "Is not this David the king of the land? did they not sing one to another of him in dances, saying, Saul hath slain his thousands, and David his ten thousands?" (I Sam. 21:11).

Hearing of this David became afraid and pretended insanity. He went so far as to let his spittle fall down upon his beard which in the east was considered the act of a madman. While walking in faith and in the fear of the Lord David had destroyed Goliath. The king of Achish, however, was no Goliath, yet David, being out of fellowship with the Lord was full of fear. Though he had the giant's sword in his possession while in Gath, it gave him no courage or reassurance. This whole trend of affairs started with doubt and ended in Gath with David being chased from the king's presence. What a poor testimony David left behind him in Gath. He was humiliated and God was dishonored.

When he fled from Gath, David escaped to the cave of Adullam. Then "when his brethren and all his father's house heard it, they went down thither to him" (I Sam. 22:1). He was back in Israel again. Hiding in the cave, he had time to think of his sin and to evaluate the mess he had gotten himself into. He must have wondered if God was through with him. David had much to learn. God permitted this testing though He was not responsible for David's actions. He used even the follies of His servant to bring him back to Himself.

If David's heart condition had been like that of Saul, this would have been the end for him. Deep down in his innermost being David wanted to do the will of God. Later, when reflecting on this sad condition, David said, "The steps of a good man are ordered by the Lord." The word, "good," is in italics, placed there by the translators. What David said was, "The steps of a man are ordered by the Lord: and he delighteth in his way. Though he fall, he shall not be utterly cast down: for the Lord upholdeth him with his hand" (Ps. 37:23,24). Another translator puts it in this way: "From God are the steps of a man made firm, when with his ways he is well pleased. Though he fall, he shall not be hurled headlong, for God is holding him up."

In verse 28 of the same Psalm we read, "For the Lord loveth judgment, and forsaketh not his saints; they are preserved for ever." This is the way God treats His children, and David is able to put it in words for us. It was while he was in the cave of Adullam that David wrote two of his most wonderful Psalms—56 and 34. These disclose what was really in his heart. Some more of his reflections are given in Psalm 118 where we read: "The Lord is on my side; I will not fear: what can man do unto me? It is better to trust in the Lord than to put confidence in man. It is better to trust in the Lord than to put confidence in princes."

The same lesson is emphasized for us in Romans 8:31,32: "If God be for us, who can be against us? He that spared not his own Son, but delivered him up for us all, how shall he not with him also freely give us all things?"

Though David was cast down, faith sprang forth to the rescue. What is in the heart of a man will eventually come out. Though David failed and sinned, he also deeply repented and his spirit was chastened. This is one of the basic differences between David and many many other men who are members of the family of God. David spoke much of trust and of mercy and of the righteousness of God. He saw that God knows our being and knows our weaknesses. God knows that we are but dust, but if we will come clean, God's mercy will endure for us.

Once more David placed his feet on the solid rock of fellowship with the Lord. He cried in Psalm 56: "Be merciful unto me, O God: for man would swallow me up; he fighting daily oppresseth me. Mine enemies would daily swallow me up: for they be many that fight against me, O thou most High. What time I am afraid, I will trust in thee. In God I will praise his word, in God I have put my trust; I will not fear what flesh can do unto me." This is the cry of a man turning back to God in deep repentance. Finally, David says, "When I cry unto thee, then shall mine enemies turn back: this I know; for God is for me. For thou hast delivered my soul from death: wilt not thou deliver my feet from falling, that I may walk before God in the light of the living?"

So David came back to the Lord. He repented before his God. He had time to reflect on his conduct as he hid in the cave, and he became thoroughly disgusted with his shameful actions. God had permitted this testing to come upon him and for a time David had failed. But when his eyes are turned back to God, we see what is really in this man's heart. No wonder he could say in Psalm 34: "I will bless the Lord at all times: his praise shall continually be in my mouth. My soul shall make her boast in the Lord: the humble shall hear thereof, and be glad. O magnify the Lord with me, and let us exalt his name together. I sought the Lord, and he heard me, and delivered me from all my fears. This poor man cried, and the Lord heard him, and saved him out of all his troubles. O taste and see that the Lord is good: blessed is the man that trusteth in him. O fear the Lord, ye his saints: for there is no want to them that fear him." This is the kind of response that made David the man after God's own heart.

CHAPTER SIX

DAVID IN REJECTION GATHERS HIS MIGHTY MEN

I Samuel 22

We find in this chapter that David has left off hiding among his enemies and has returned to his own land. It was during this period in his experience that he wrote Psalms 34, 57 and 142.

While he was in the cave of Adullam "his brethren and all his father's house heard it, and they went down thither to him. And every one that was in distress, and every one that was in debt, and every one that was discontented, gathered themselves unto him; and he became a captain over them: and there were with him about four hundred men" (vv. 1,2). This placed a great deal of responsibility on David's shoulders, his first responsibility being the safety of his parents. It was then that David went to Mizpeh in Moab and said to the king of Moab, "Let my father and my mother, I pray thee, come forth, and be with you, till I know what God will do for me." This was more like the David of old. His circumstances were troubled and full of distress, but he himself was looking to see what God would do for him.

David was naturally concerned for his parents knowing that since Saul had outlawed him, the king would seek vengeance on them if the opportunity presented itself. David undoubtedly took them to Mizpeh of Moab because his great grandmother, Ruth the Moabitess, came from there. He very likely knew relatives in that area willing to give Jesse and his family asylum.

In all of this it is evident that David had no animosity against his family even though he had been treated as less than a son in his early years. He was not of a vindicative nature. He was not a man to carry a grudge.

After David had found a safe place for his parents, the Prophet Gad said to him, "Abide not in the hold; depart, and get thee into the land of Judah. Then David departed, and came into the forest of Hareth" (v. 5).

David was still a fugitive but he was no longer out of step with God. He walked in obedience and fellowship with God. Let us not forget that the same Holy Spirit who was controlling David's life at this time was also the Spirit who filled without measure the life of our Saviour during His life on earth. He is the same Holy Spirit who indwells those of us today who have trusted in Christ for salvation. What the Holy Spirit did for David He can do for us. David awaited God's time and did not in any wise seek to usurp the authority of Saul or to depose him by force. He left all that in God's hands.

David trained and disciplined the men who made up his small army until they formed the core of the greatest army Israel ever had. They eventually won for their nation the greatest victories it ever enjoyed. These men came from various backgrounds. Some were bankrupts, some possibly were discontented with this lot in life. One might be tempted to think that they would never amount to much as a group or as individuals. But when we turn to such passages as II Samuel 23 and I Chronicles 11 where the remarkable military achievements of these men are recounted, we are forced to realize that they were an unusual band.

It is also true that they had an unusual captain who took the responsibility of training them as soldiers by first of all training them as believers. In the 34th Psalm David says, "Come [talking to these men] . . . I will teach you the fear of the Lord." This was no theory with David, but actual experience. He had run from God. During that time of backsliding he doubted God, told lies and feared man. But that time is past. Now he is in fellowship with God once more. He had come clean with God and rested in Him with greater confidence and trust than ever before.

David was God's anointed king in exile. These men gathered around him, recognizing him as God's chosen one. They were willing to await God's time with him, and willing if necessary to suffer with him. They did for David what we are admonished to do for Christ in Hebrews 13: "Let us go forth therefore unto him without the camp, bearing his reproach." Paul reminds us in Romans 8:17: We are "heirs of God, and joint-heirs with Christ; if so be that we suffer with him." Our Lord is now rejected but is gathering together a group to reign with Him. This is only a small army. They are equipped to fight not with carnal weapons but with the spiritual weapons which are mighty through God. With Christ as Captain this army will conquer.

We can only do great things in the future as we learn to do the right things now. We learn from Ephesians 2:5,6 that we have been "raised up together, and made to sit together in heavenly places in Christ Jesus." This is something that is true of us now. We are being trained by our Lord now and can learn to say as did Paul, "I can do all things through Christ which strengtheneth me."

God intends us to enjoy victory over our enemies now as well as in the future. The 19th chapter of the Book of Revelation depicts one of the greatest of future victories. The largest army that men have ever assembled will seek to overthrow God. He will send Christ with His trained ones—you and I who have been with Christ—to overcome the enemy. Here is what the Scriptures tell us: "And I saw heaven opened, and behold a white horse; and he that sat upon him was called Faithful and True, and in righteousness he doth judge and make war. His eyes were as a flame of fire, and on his head were many crowns; and he had a name written, that no man knew, but he himself." He does not appear alone for we learn: "And the armies which were in heaven followed him upon white horses, clothed in fine linen, white and clean. And out of his mouth goeth a sharp sword, that with it he should smite the nations: and he shall rule them with a rod of iron."

Our faithfulness now will bring us reward then, for we are told: "But that which ye have already hold fast till I come. And he that overcometh, and keepeth my works unto the end, to him will I give power over the nations: And he shall rule them with a rod of iron; as the vessels of a potter shall they be broken to shivers: even as I received of my Father" (Rev. 2:25-27). And still a further promise is given in Revelation 3:21: "To him that overcometh will I grant to sit with me in my throne, even as I also overcame, and am set down with my Father in his throne."

David taught his men first of all to fear the Lord for this is the beginning of wisdom. These were troubled men, and he taught them of the God who delivers His people out of all their troubles. Some of these men were being unjustly dealt with. They were distressed, so David introduced them to the Lord who hears the cry of those seeking righteousness and justice. They were men who, like David, had their problems with sin. For this reason he taught them the fear of the Lord who is near to them who are of a broken heart and saves such as are of a contrite spirit.

Some of these men were bankrupts and rather than sell themselves to either Saul or Achish to be slaves, they chose rejection with David.

What was the motive that underlay their decision? They saw beyond the present distress David was in and believed God's promises concerning David's future exaltation. Saul was king, but he was rejected of God though he held on to the throne by force. These men who had come to be with David looked beyond to the time when God's will would be accomplished.

A greater than David calls us to submit ourselves to Him. He is asking for our allegiance. If we deny Him that allegiance and suffering now, He will deny us the reigning later on. Learn to be a good and obedient soldier for Jesus Christ now, and He will exalt you in due time.

CHAPTER SEVEN

DAVID LEARNS TO COUNSEL WITH GOD

I Samuel 23

The life of David is a very instructive life for the believer. The Bible gives us such a complete picture of his life, both the good and the bad, that we can draw much help from his experiences. From the experiences in the 23rd chapter of I Samuel we will find how David learned to seek the will of God. The pursuit of this knowledge was not new to David, but in his previous experiences he had allowed personal reasoning to conflict with God's instructions and this brought serious troubles.

We have already seen that Gad the prophet had joined David's forces and had communicated God's instructions to David with reference to his safety. He was no longer to hide in a cave of Adullam but to dwell in the hilly and forest country of Judah. David learned that God is our God forever and ever and that He will be our guide even unto death. Such a lesson, however, is not learned overnight.

News was brought to David that the Philistines had come against a city called Keilah. Some of the warfare we read of in these chapters in I Samuel was very much like guerrilla warfare of the present day. These bands of Philistines ranged the country like predatory beasts. The favorite time for their raids was right at the harvest when the grain had been brought to the threshing floors. This was the spoils these bands were after.

When David learned of the coming Philistine invasion, he

asked the Lord saying, "Shall I go and smite these Philistines? And the Lord said unto David, Go, and smite the Philistines, and save Keilah." In spite of the fact that David was being hunted and persecuted, he loved his own people and was not so engrossed in his own problems that he forgot theirs. The important thing for David, of course, was to seek God's will in every detail. He had learned by costly mistakes that his own unassisted reasoning was not sufficient to guide him through the troubles of life.

David found that he had more than himself to consider in these matters. Because he was the captain of a band of men, he had to give thought to their reactions and seek to lead them in the way that God was leading him. His men said to him when he decided to go against Keilah: "Behold, we be afraid here in Judah: how much more then if we come to Keilah against the armies of the Philistines?" (v. 3). The problem was that if they went against the Philistines, Saul might come against them and they would be caught between two fires. It was this that provided David the opportunity of teaching them some of the marvelous things of God.

It was not to be expected that they would go into this battle on David's faith alone. We do not exercise victory on the basis of another man's faith. They could no more live on David's faith than we can live on the faith of another human being. We must live by the faith that God gives. Our Lord's admonition in Mark 11:22 is to "have faith in God." This is possible because Galatians 2:20 tells us: "Nevertheless I live; yet not I but Christ liveth in me: and the life which I now live in the flesh I live by the faith of the Son of God, who loved me, and gave himself for me." It is Christ living in each believer who creates this faith in each one.

Finding his men reluctant to go to the aid of Keilah, David inquired of the Lord once more, and the Lord answered him by saying, "Arise, go down to Keilah; for I will deliver the Philistines into thine hand." In this second inquiry the same answer is given but now the men are taught to believe in God personally and directly. In obedience to this word, "David and his men went to Keilah." These men not only heard but they did what the Word said. It is not those who hear only but the doers of the Word with whom God is pleased. Not everyone who says, "Lord, Lord, shall enter into the kingdom of heaven; but he that doeth the will of my Father" (Matt. 7:24). And he who does "the will of God shall abide forever" the Word tells us. Obedience then, is the thing that is of uttermost importance with regard to the directions of God. The obedience must follow clear on through the final details.

God delivered the enemy into the hands of David and his men. David saved the inhabitants of the city and at the same time captured the cattle and the other foodstuffs the Philistines had brought along for their own use. So David not only defeated the enemy but gained much needed food supplies for his men. It is when we are obedient that God is able to supply our needs above all that we can ask or think.

We learn also from this chapter that men who intend evil can also speak of the Lord and His work in a very pious way. Saul was told that David had delivered Keilah and Saul said, "God hath delivered him into mine hand; for he is shut in, by entering into a town that hath gates and bars." This was Saul speaking, a man who had been so disobedient to God that the Spirit of God had departed from him. He was a man who, no matter how he prayed, received no answer from God, because his heart was not right toward God. Yet, here he was saying that God had delivered David into his hands.

We must always be careful of our interpretation of circumstances. On a number of occasions I have counseled with different persons who were very obviously following a selfish path. Their one strong argument was that the circumstances looked favorable to the course they wanted to take; but it was obvious to me, at least, that they were viewing circumstances in a false light. I was able to check the subsequent history of some of these persons and found them miserable in heart with no joy in the Lord. If our wills are not wholly given over to the Lord, we are bound to misinterpret the circumstances around us.

The Lord had not given David into Saul's hands and was already providing the means of escape for His servant. David knew of Saul's base intentions and asked Abiathar, the priest, who had joined him at Keilah, to bring out the ephod. This David used in asking the Lord what he should do. David prayed, "O Lord God of Israel, thy servant hath certainly heard that Saul seeketh to come to Keilah, to destroy the city for my sake. Will the men of Keilah deliver me up into his hands? will Saul come down, as thy servant hath heard? O Lord God of Israel, I beseech thee, tell thy servant. And the Lord said, He will come down. Then said David, Will the men of Keilah deliver me and my men into the hand of Saul? And the Lord said, They will deliver thee up" (vv. 10-12).

With this information David and his 600 men lost no time in making their exit from Keilah.

David sought God's mind in every step. Psalm 25 fits into this particular picture very well. In verse 14 David said, "The secret of the Lord is with them that fear him; and he will show them his covenant." This word "fear" means "reverential trust" in God, with a hatred for evil. In another part of the Psalm David said, "Show me thy way, O Lord, teach me thy path." Showing may be by pointing, but teaching is often done through experience. David continued, "Lead me in thy truth, and teach me: for thou art the God of my salvation; on thee do I wait all the day. Remember, O Lord, thy tender mercies and thy loving-kindnesses; for they have been ever of old. Remember not the sins of my youth, nor my transgressions: according to thy mercy remember thou me for thy goodness' sake, O Lord. Good and upright is the Lord: therefore will he teach sinners in the way. The meek will he guide in judgment: and the meek will he teach his way. All the paths of the Lord are mercy, and truth unto such as keep his covenant and his testimonies. For thy name's sake, O Lord, pardon mine iniquity; for it is great. What man is he that feareth the Lord? him shall he teach in the way that he shall choose." Then follows a description of what the blessings are that a man enjoys who follows in the way of the Lord. David said, "His soul shall dwell at ease; and his seed shall inherit the earth."

In concluding the Psalm David prayed: "O keep my soul, and deliver me: let me not be ashamed; for I put my trust in thee. Let integrity and uprightness preserve me; for I wait on thee" (vv. 20,21). Waiting on the Lord is one of the difficulties we experience because we have the tendency to become impatient under trial. We do not like to wait especially if our own time is involved. Waiting, however, is not necessarily an element of time, it may be a matter of distinguishing the voice of the Lord from other voices. There are some musicians who can tell if a member of a quartet or choir has missed a note or sounded a wrong note. This calls for a carefully trained ear, the very thing the Lord wants us to have in the spiritual realm.

In order to make this matter of finding the Lord's will practical to us in this day and age, we need to examine more closely some of the principles involved in David's learning the will of God. Look again at verse 9: "And David knew that Saul secretly practised mischief against him; and he said to Abiathar the priest, Bring hither the ephod." This man, you will recall, was the only member of the priestly house of Eli who escaped from the massacre instituted by Saul. Abiathar brought with him the ephod which was some kind of cloak that the priest of Israel wore. The high priest also wore a breastplate which contained 12 stones, each stone representing one of the tribes of Israel. Then there were stones called the urim and thummim by which the will of God was ascertained. Just how this was done is not clear though some Old Testament scholars believe that the priests would pray to God and ask the necessary questions. If the answer was "Yes," the stones would shine brilliantly, but if the answer was "No," the stones would become darkened.

There were other means God used to let men know His will, but a rebellious man like Saul received no answer from

God at all. In the 28th chapter of I Samuel we learn that the Philistines brought a great army against Saul. He was terrified and inquired of the Lord what he should do. "The Lord answered him not, neither by dreams, nor by Urim, nor by prophets." The situation with David was altogether different. He sought not only to know the will of God but to do it.

In this connection it is of interest to see what God gives the overcomer according to the second chapter of the Book of Revelation. There we read in verse 17: "He that hath an ear, let him hear what the Spirit saith unto the churches; To him that overcometh will I give to eat of the hidden manna, and will give him a white stone, and in the stone a new name written, which no man knoweth saving he that receiveth it." The actual translation of "stone" should be "a brilliant shining stone." The person receiving this stone will know that he has the approval of God. This is God's "Yes" to the overcomer. He is the man who has heard the Lord say, "This is the way, walk ye in it" and has obeyed.

Our High Priest who now intercedes for us at the throne of God will help us through His Spirit and the Word to know the will of God. God does not send us visions or give us a urim and thummin to consult, but He gives us illumination in our souls and joy as we walk in His will. There will only be darkness to the person whose life is stained with sin or who is rebelling against God.

A guided life is dependent upon a cleansed heart. "If we say we have fellowship with him, and walk in darkness, we lie, and do not the truth: But if we walk in the light, as he is in the light, we have fellowship one with another, and the blood of Jesus Christ his Son cleanseth us from all sin" (I John 1:6,7). James tells us, "If any man lack wisdom, let him ask of God that giveth to all men liberally, and upbraideth not; and it shall be given him. But let him ask in faith, nothing wavering. For he that wavereth is like a wave of the sea driven with the wind and tossed. Let not that man think that he shall receive any thing of the Lord. A double minded man is unstable in all his ways."

Do we want to know the will of God and do we want to know the purpose God has in a certain circumstance or situation in our lives? Then let us ask God for wisdom. If we want it for the purpose of continuing in the will of God, He will give it to us. On the other hand, if we want it so that we might sit in judgment and decide whether we want to do the will of God or not, then God will not show us. It is to the man who is willing to do the will of God that God reveals His mind (John 7:17).

According to I Thessalonians 5:3-8, we are the children of light and are not to walk in darkness as though we were children of darkness. The light, of course, is the Word of God.

David in Psalm 25 shows us how he continually waited on God and asked God for direction for his life. "O my God, I will trust in thee: let me not be ashamed, let not mine enemies triumph over me. I will wait on thee. Shew me thy ways, O Lord; teach me thy paths. Lead me in thy truth, and teach me thy way and I will wait for thee."

Along with this David asked for cleansing from sin. He prayed that God would not remember the sins of his youth, nor his transgressions. David found it was the meek that the Lord guided in judgment and to whom He taught His ways. He found that all the paths of the Lord were merciful and truth for him. David asked for pardon for his iniquity and asserted, as we have seen in another place, that "the secret of the Lord is with them that fear him; and he will show him his covenant. Mine eyes are ever toward the Lord; and he shall pluck my feet out of the net." David found that the troubles of his heart were enlarged and prayed that God would bring him out of them all. He cried, "Look to my afflictions and forgive my sins." David wanted to do the will of God; that was why he asked that he might know it.

David learned from the Lord that the people of Keilah would deliver him over to Saul so he went to Ziph to his own kinsmen but found them unfaithful. It is heartbreaking for a man to learn that his foes are sometimes those of his own household.

These tribesmen of David sent word to Saul that David was hiding in their country and they promised to deliver him to the king. Saul said, "Blessed be ye of the Lord; for ye have compassion on me" (v. 21). Once again the hypocrisy of Saul's language shows up. Saul took a group of soldiers with him and sought out David and pursued him. Apparently Saul thought he had David cornered when a messenger brought word that the Philistines had invaded the land.

CHAPTER EIGHT

LOVE YOUR ENEMIES

I Samuel 24

It is of great comfort to know that God will move whole armies if necessary to deliver a child of His from the hands of His enemies. When all seemed lost, God permitted the Philistines to invade the land of Israel so Saul had to leave off hunting David and go to fight the invaders.

This soon brings David into another test on a different level than he had met before. Would David really trust God under any kind of circumstance to bring him to the throne of Israel without raising his hand in any way to remove Saul?

No sooner had Saul dealt with the Philistines than he turned and followed David into the wilderness of En-gedi. With an army of three thousand picked men, Saul went into the area of the rocks of the wild goats. "He came to the sheep-cotes by the way, where was a cave; and Saul went in to cover his feet: and David and his men remained in the sides of the cave." The situation is not hard to grasp. Saul was not as young as he once was and, no doubt, the area of En-gedi was very hot. It was close to the Dead Sea which is some 1400 feet below the level of the Mediterranean. Saul decided he needed a rest and entered the cave for the benefit of its quietness and coolness. He did not know that David and his men were hiding in the recesses of that particular cave.

Leaving most or all of his men outside, Saul carelessly entered and lay down and dropped off to sleep. To David's men this was his opportunity to rid himself of Saul. They thought it was a God-given opportunity, but David did not agree. "The men of David said unto him, Behold the day of which the Lord said unto thee, Behold, I will deliver thine enemy into thine hand, that thou mayest do to him as it shall seem good unto thee. Then David arose, and cut off the skirt of Saul's robe privily."

David's men jumped at the conclusion that these circumstances were God-made for David to take the life of Saul. They even quoted from one of David's favorite Psalms, "Behold, I will deliver thine enemy into thine hand," to back up their argument. It does not take a strong imagination to picture how they must have argued and pleaded with him to get rid of his enemy once and for all. It would mean an end to their hardships and suffering. It would mean that David would have the throne for himself and would rid the land of its apostasy and idolatry. Like many in our day, they very probably believed that the end justified the means. They possibly believed that for David to kill Saul would be carrying out the will of God. This would bring rest and peace to their country and especially to David and the men who had followed with him. We can see from this that the test before David was no small one.

With regard to the subject of testings, I Corinthians 10:13 gives us a basic principle: "There hath no temptation [test] taken you but such as is common to man: but God is faithful, who will not suffer you to be tempted [tested] above that ye are able; but will with the temptation [test] also make a way to escape." David was faced with a new kind of test for him, and yet it was a test that believers often meet.

Had David reasoned about this—and he possibly did—he would recognize that this was a golden opportunity for him to get rid of his enemy. But David had been learning that reason alone was not sufficient. He decided to wait on God. What his men urged could be true, but it would be at the sacrifice of faith and at the sacrifice of a humble will that was submissive to God. If David took matters into his own hands now, it would be at the expense of a thousand precious experiences of God's care, provision, guidance and tenderness. "No," reasoned David, "even a throne at that price is too dear." Faith will always wait upon God.

Even a deeper lesson must be learned from this. We need to be exceedingly cautious how we interpret what we call God's providences, drawing our own conclusions from them rather than waiting to see God's purposes back of them. It is true that David had cried for deliverance. The Psalms are very clear on that. He not only cried for deliverance, he also cried for justice and vindication. Here is how he prayed in Psalm 54: "Save me, O God, by thy name, and judge me by thy strength. For he hath delivered me out of all trouble: and mine eye hath seen his desire upon mine enemies." But this was not all that David had seen with regard to the Lord. He knew the truth that was later stated for us in the New Testament in the words: "Recompense to no man evil for evil. Provide things honest in the sight of all men. If it be possible, as much as lieth in you, live peaceably with all men. Dearly beloved, avenge not yourselves, but rather give place unto wrath: for it is written, Vengeance is mine; I will repay, saith the Lord. Therefore if thine enemy hunger, feed him; if he thirst, give him drink: for in so doing thou shalt heap coals of fire on his head. Be not overcome with evil, but overcome evil with good" (Rom. 12:17-21).

Our Lord said in Matthew 5:44: "But I say unto you, Love your enemies, bless them that curse you, do good to them that hate you, and pray for them which despitefully use you, and persecute you." David was learning the truth of these verses even though they had not yet been recorded in the Scriptures. David was being tested as to his faith and his patience and his piety. "Will God do it?" This was the test of his faith. "The time will come when God will set me on the throne of Israel"—this was the test of his patience. He would wait for God's time. "What should a man of God do toward his enemy?" This is where David's piety was tested. David recognized that though Saul was in the wrong, he was still God's anointed. And for David this was the answer to his men. He said, "The Lord forbid that I should do this thing unto my master, the Lord's anointed, to stretch forth mine hand against him, seeing he is the anointed of the Lord." Though rejected, Saul was still the king of Israel, and David would not raise his hand against his king.

God has a time for everything, and it is always better to wait God's time. God was longsuffering with Saul. He had been longsuffering with Israel for 38 years in the desert. How long has God been longsuffering with us? Sometimes it is difficult to wait God's time, but it takes time to build character.

When Israel felt themselves trapped at the Red Sea, they were told not to run or to rush but to stand still and see the salvation of the Lord. This is not an easy lesson to learn, but it is a needed one. David was a man after the heart of God because he did God's will. So as David waited, God molded his character. David would not have been the writer of 73 or more wonderful Psalms had he not waited for God's time under severe testing. He waited eight years under Saul before being crowned king of Judah. Then he had to wait seven more years before he gained the allegiance of all the tribes of Israel.

Rather than take Saul's life, David merely cut off a portion of Saul's skirt. But even that apparently touched David's conscience, for we read that his "heart smote him." A tender conscience is a good thing when God controls it. David realized what an indignity he had imposed on a king. But a tender conscience made tender by God is a mark of spirituality. Too many have their consciences seared as with a hot iron and are past feeling. Paul expressed the desire of the true believer when he said, "that I might have a conscience clear before God and men." This was the attitude of David.

David confessed his feelings not only to God but also to his men. This took grace and courage, but it was necessary to help keep his fellowship to God open. David found no trouble in persuading his men that what he did in not taking

Saul's life was right. It is when people see the reality in our lives of what we say that they are persuaded we are walking in the way of the Lord.

When Saul awoke, he left the cave not knowing how near to death he had been. In fact, the only reason he left the cave alive was that the man whose life he sought was a man who had a heart that pleased God and sought to do the will of God.

David waited until Saul was a safe distance away then called to him, bowing to the ground before him. David did not cringe before his king as a criminal, but bowed as a loyal subject who had nothing to hide. Then he uttered one of the most respectful, forceful, and yet soul-touching addresses ever made to one of earth's rulers. In it he asked Saul some questions. One is, "Wherefore hearest thou men's words, saying, Behold, David seeketh thy hurt?" The words of lying talebearers can be deadly. Words may not take a man's physical life, but they can often murder his character. What is our attitude under such circumstances?

David reminded Saul that in listening to these talebearers he was listening to men and not to God, a very unwise thing to do.

Then he gave evidence of his good intentions toward Saul. He said, "Behold, this day thine eyes have seen how that the Lord had delivered thee to day into mine hand in the cave." And then he held up the piece of cloth that he had cut from Saul's garment as a visible exhibition that he could just as easily have cut off Saul's head.

We can surely learn from this that to get even with someone who has wronged us is not in the will of God for His people. The man who walks in fellowship with God will not seek personal revenge.

It is doubtful if God would test many of us like this, for it is unlikely that we would pass it. The Scripture says, "He will not test us above that we are able." But if we are not tested in this way, we are not victors in this way either. And in this line of development, we will remain feeble.

David continued asking Saul questions to help bring that

monarch's mind to a true appreciation of what he was doing in hunting David. "After whom is the king of Israel come out? after whom dost thou pursue? after a dead dog, after a flea?" David's evaluation of himself is not very high. Though he has been chosen of God and anointed to be king of Israel, he still is not on the throne and his own spirit is that of humility and not of pride. Once a flea is caught, it is not worth much; and yet it is not easy to catch because it is first here and then there and then somewhere else. And that was Saul's experience in trying to catch David. Had Saul succeeded, he would have destroyed someone who in his own opinion was nothing better than a dead dog or a flea.

David had committed himself and his case to the Lord. In the words of Psalm 37:5,6 he had trusted in the Lord knowing that He would bring it to pass. David also learned: "And he shall bring forth thy righteousness as the light, and thy judgment as the noonday." God will vindicate His own people.

When Paul's character was maligned in Corinth, he wrote to that church saying: "So you must stop forming any premature judgments, and wait until the Lord shall come again; for He will bring to light the secrets hidden in the dark and will make known the motives of men's hearts, and the proper praise shall be awarded each of us" (I Cor. 4:5, Williams). We need to learn from this to leave our case with the Lord as did David. He did not even seek to vindicate himself, much less revenge himself. He left it all with the Lord.

The following Scriptures will help us see where true greatness lies. "He that is slow to anger is better than the mighty; and he that ruleth his spirit than he that taketh a city" (Prov. 16:32). "A soft answer turneth away wrath: but grievous words stir up anger" (Prov. 15:1). This passage from the New Testament will help us also. "The wisdom that is from above is first pure, then peaceable, gentle, and easy to be intreated, full of mercy and good fruits, without partiality, and without hypocrisy" (James 3:17). We are also admonished to forebear "one another, forgiving one another, if any man have a quarrel against any: even as Christ forgave you, so also do ye" (Col. 3:13). To cap all this is Proverbs 24:29: "Say not, I will do so to him as he hath done to me: I will render to the man according to his work," or as it is stated in Romans 12:21, "Be not overcome of evil, but overcome evil with good."

When Saul realized how close he had come to death and how David's integrity had kept his hand from off his life, the king said, "Thou art more righteous than I." He continued, "Thou hast rewarded me good, whereas I have rewarded thee evil. And thou hast shewed this day how that thou hast dealt well with me: forasmuch as when the Lord had delivered me into thine hand, thou killedst me not. For if a man find his enemy, will he let him go well away?" Saul knew that what David had done was something that he himself would not have done. Rankling in Saul's mind all the time is this: "Behold, I know well that thou shalt surely be king, and that the kingdom of Israel shall be established in thine hand." Though momentarily Saul is stopped in his evil intentions, he has not bowed his heart to the will of God with regard to David succeeding him on the throne.

This also goes to show that when a man will honor God, God will honor him. In this connection Proverbs 16:7 is very fitting: "When a man's ways please the Lord, he maketh even his enemies to be at peace with him."

Saul not only recognized that David would be Israel's next king, but he also knew that if David acted as many kings did, he might possibly destroy the entire family of Saul. So he, knowing he could trust David's integrity, said according to verse 21: "Swear now therefore unto me by the Lord, that thou wilt not cut off my seed after me, and that thou wilt not destroy my name out of my father's house."

Will our character stand a test like this? Will our enemies be able to rest in our promises as Saul did on David's? Unbelievers have often had good reason to point an accusing finger at Christians for their lack of consistent living. Some Christians have even observed that it is easier at times to work with men of the world than it is to work with some professing Christians. If others should ever have reason to distrust us, the fault will lie in our failure to keep a proper relationship with God.

David, of course, first gained the victory over himself before he triumphed over Saul. This is not done at a church altar though we can make very momentous decisions there. The decisions are only the opening of the door to a life of walking in victory with God. The life of victory is something that is accomplished through a moment by moment fellowship with God.

We see something of David's private talking with God in such a Psalm as Psalm 56. There David cried: "Be merciful unto me, O God: for man would swallow me up; he fighting daily oppresseth me." It was through this type of communication with God that David first won the victory over himself. He had to win there before his enemies came to respect him and to place their trust in him. He continues: "Mine enemies would daily swallow me up: for they be many that fight against me, O thou most High. What time I am afraid, I will trust in thee. In God I will praise his word, in God I have put my trust; I will not fear what flesh can do unto me. Every day they wrest my words: all their thoughts are against me for evil. They gather themselves together, they hide themselves, they mark my steps, when they wait for my soul." In all of this, David lays out before the Lord the things that are disturbing his mind and heart.

At the conclusion David says to the Lord: "For thou hast delivered my soul from death: wilt not thou deliver my feet from falling, that I may walk before the Lord in the light of the living?" This is the key to it all. David says that God has saved him and kept him from being destroyed by the wicked. Now he wants his feet to be kept from falling. He committed himself into God's hands for this.

In Psalm 57:7,8 David says, "My heart is fixed, O God, my heart is fixed: I will sing and give praise, Awake up, my glory; awake, psaltery and harp."

David Confronts a Fool, I Samuel 25

David does not shine so well in the following incident as he did with regard to Saul. This is a dark picture that is presented to us but, as we have noted before, God does not gloss over the sins of his people. Most biographers would be inclined to leave out this chapter in David's life, but the Holy Spirit is not afraid to reveal what is in the heart. Here was the case where David was a miserable failure though even in his failure we catch a glimpse of why God called him a man after his own heart. There is no thought of belittling David's sin in this case, for when confronted with it, he meets it as only a believer can who has had previous fellowship with God. Here we will see how God delights to work against a background of seeming hopelessness in the human heart.

God does not condone sin. He exposes it and will cleanse it from the hearts of those who are willing to be cleansed. We need to see what we are by nature. In seeing the carnal heart of David in this incident we see the depravity of man, contrasted with the infinite wisdom and mercy of God. There is a contrast here between David's victory as he controlled his temper according to chapter 24 and this miserable failure when he completely lost his temper as recounted in chapter 25. In the former chapter we see him leaving vengeance to God, but in this one we see him about to take vengeance into his own hands.

David could well praise God for having delivered his soul from death. He could also pray with real fervor, asking that his feet be kept from falling and that he might walk before God in the light of the living. Fitting right in with this is a statement by a missionary now with the Lord: "Walk softly, speak tenderly, pray fervently." This would have been a good motto for David in the following experience. It is always a good motto for us.

We meet two new characters in this 25th chapter of I Samuel. One is Nabal, and the other is his wife Abigail. The Scripture says of her that she was "a woman of good understanding, and of a beautiful countenance: but the man was churlish and evil in his doings; and he was of the house of Caleb."

While David and his men had been hiding from Saul in the southern part of the land of Canaan, they were not idle. They contributed in a great measure to the peace and security of the people in that area. Those were troubled days and roving bands of Philistines and others would molest the sheepherders and farmers in the outlying districts and try to rob them of their flocks, herds and grain. David with his 600 men was very active in protecting these Israelites. Though hiding from Saul, David was also performing a real service to his country and people. This, of course, helped him to win a place in their hearts. In the providence of God David's years as a hunted man were contributing to his popularity among the Israelites.

It was no easy task to provide food for 600 men as active as David's men were. They were in no position to raise their own food, but since they protected the farmers in that area, it was apparently the understanding that the farmers would contribute to the support of this garrison. The fact is, without them many of the people of that vicinity would have lost everything they had to Israel's enemies. Thus it was with some confidence that David sent ten of his young men to Nabal to greet him, to wish him prosperity and peace, and to ask him to help provide food for David's band. They had helped Nabal's herders in particular and had taken nothing from them by way of compensation.

Nabal, though a descendant of Caleb, was a poor representative of that noble line. The name "Nabal" means fool and that is just how he acted.

Nabal answered David's servants and said, "Who is David? and who is the son of Jesse? there be many servants now a days that break away every man from his master. Shall I then take my bread, and my water, and my flesh that I have killed for my shearers, and give it unto men, whom I know not whence they be?" He acted as though he did not know who David was, though he undoubtedly knew a good deal about David but was using this method of showing his contempt. The man was exceedingly selfish and did not want to give to anyone even though he had an overabundance for himself. He tried to justify his actions by inferring that David's men were rebels who did not care to be tied down to responsibilities of home or government. This was an insult that David felt keenly.

Let me apply this to a situation that is altogether too common in our own day. There are many faith works, missionary and otherwise not controlled by some particular denomination, that look to the Lord and then to His people for support for the work that God has given them to do. But then along comes a strong organized group and some of their preachers say, "Who are these faith works? What are they doing? We have no control over them so why should we allow our people to give to their work?" Let me leave this subject with just one question: "Who is the Lord of the harvest, anyway?"

Nabal's niggardly attitude was made known to David by his ten young messengers. Then it was that David lost his temper. He armed 400 of his band and left 200 to guard the stuff. David said, "Surely in vain have I kept all that this fellow hath in the wilderness, so that nothing was missed of all that pertained unto him: and he hath requited me evil for good. So and more also do God unto the enemies of David, if I leave of all that pertain to him" (vv. 21,22). David was so angry that he was ready to destroy Nabal's entire family.

In the meantime, one of Nabal's servants came to Abigail and related to her the coming of the ten young messengers from David and Nabal's harsh words to them. This young man assured Abigail that David's men had protected Nabal's property so that not a thing was taken. He said to her, "They were a wall unto us both by night and day, all the while we were with them keeping the sheep" (v. 16).

This young man spoke very frankly to his master's wife and said, "Now therefore know and consider what thou wilt do; for evil is determined against our master, and against all his household: for he is such a son of Belial, that a man cannot speak to him" (v. 17).

David did not meet this testing as he had met the testing concerning Saul. Then he was gracious and noble and kind hearted, but now he is ready to destroy a whole family. David might have said, "That is my business. I protected this man; I kept him and his servants from harm, and protected his herds and his goods, and now he returns evil for good. He is not going to get by with it. It was all right when Saul was after me, for Saul was God's anointed, but who is this fellow? I will teach him a lesson."

Abigail was of different stuff than her husband. She decided to do what her husband failed to do and had donkeys loaded up with all kinds of food and then went out to meet David.

When she saw him, "She hasted, and lighted off the ass, and fell down before David on her face, and bowed herself to the ground, And fell at his feet, and said, Upon me, my lord, upon me let this iniquity be." Here is true intercession. She did not want this sin to be put on her husband who had acted as a fool acts; she wanted to bear the responsibility for this wrong.

She continued her plea with the words, "Let not my lord, I pray thee, regard this man of Belial, even Nabal: for as his name is, so is he; Nabal is his name, and folly is with him: but I thine handmaid saw not the young men of my lord, whom thou didst send. Now therefore, my lord, as the Lord liveth, and as thy soul liveth, seeing the Lord hath withholden thee from coming to shed blood, and from avenging thyself with thine own hand, now let thine enemies, and they that seek evil to my lord, be as Nabal" (vv. 25,26).

She recognized that David was out fighting the Lord's battles and that he had a right to be incensed against Nabal for his churlishness and selfishness and greed. Nevertheless she pleaded: "But the soul of my lord shall be bound in the bundle of life with the Lord thy God; and the souls of thine enemies, them shall he sling out, as out of the middle of a sling." This is the very message David needed. While he walked with God in humility, he was able in the power of the Holy Spirit with just a sling and a stone to kill Goliath and save the army of Saul from defeat. How much better it would be to leave this in God's hands and not have to look back on this experience with shame.

David admitted his fault and said to Abigail, "Blessed be the Lord God of Israel, which sent thee this day to meet me: And blessed be thy advice, and blessed be thou, which hast kept me this day from coming to shed blood, and from avenging myself with mine own hand. For in very deed, as the Lord God of Israel liveth, which hath kept me back from hurting thee, except thou hadst hasted and come to meet me, surely there had not been left unto Nabal by the morning light any" male member of the family.

David received from her hand the things she had brought, and he said to her, "Go up in peace to thine house; see, I have hearkened to thy voice, and have accepted thy person."

When Abigail returned home she found Nabal feasting like a king and very drunk. In the morning when he was sober, she told him of what had transpired the day before. Apparently he was so shocked at how close he had come to death that he became ill and died within ten days.

God did not permit David to fulfil his basic intention of killing all the males belonging to the house of Nabal. God used Abigail to perform this special service to David and to bring him back into fellowship once again with God. This should remind us that our victory of yesterday is not sufficient for today. We must have a moment by moment walk with the Lord so that as each testing comes we will come through victoriously for Christ.

Can the World See Jesus in You?

Do we live so close to the Lord today,
  Passing to and fro on life's busy way,
That the world in us can a likeness see
  To the man of Calvary?

As an open book they our lives will read,
  To our words and acts giving daily heed;
Will they be attracted, or turn away
  From the Christ we love today?

CHAPTER NINE

DAVID LEARNS OBEDIENCE

I Samuel 26

Testings may be varied, but they may also be very similar. In the chapter before this we saw David tested in a manner very much like the test he met successfully two years before. Here again he has the opportunity to take the life of Saul if he so desires. The circumstances are in some respects alike and yet in others they are not. There was need for more faith and more confidence in the Lord the second time than the first time. On the first occasion Saul had stopped inside a cave to rest during the heat of the day. He left his soldiers outside not knowing that David and many of his men were hiding in the recesses of the cave. In this second situation Saul is still in pursuit of David whose whereabouts had once again been betrayed by the Ziphites. Saul had 3000 men with him and Abner as their captain. According to verse 5, Saul lay in a trench and the people camped round about him. No doubt, he was not taking any chances and thought he was perfectly safe in the midst of the host. He reckoned, however, without God who had another lesson to teach him as well as a lesson for David.

Saul had not gotten over his jealousy. It came over him again and again because he did not judge it properly as sin. This was one of the factors which made such a great difference between Saul and David. David thoroughly judged his sin. Read for example, the 51st Psalm which was written several years following this incident and this truth will stand out. If we do not do something about sin, we will end in more sin and ultimately in death. This is the thought in Romans 8:13 where we learn: "For if ye live after the flesh, ye shall die: but if ye through the spirit do mortify [make die] the deeds of the body, ye shall live."

David sent out his spies who returned with the information that Saul and his men were gathered in a certain valley. David himself investigated to make sure that he knew where Saul was camped. He saw that Saul was in the center of the little army with Abner by his side. It was not long until they were all asleep.

David was walking with God at this time and it is not presuming to believe that he prayed to God concerning Saul being so near to him. David had completely judged the sins in his life. There was no cloud between him and his Saviour. He asked for volunteers to go with him into the camp of Saul and Abishai agreed to go with him. They carefully approached the sleeping men and made their way around them to where Saul was lying sound asleep. This could not have been possible save only that the Scriptures tell us God had caused a deep sleep to fall on Saul and his men.

David had taught his men two years previous to this episode that it was not right to kill God's anointed. But Abishai looked on this as a deliverance by God into David's hands and that Saul's life should be taken. Abishai offered to do this for David, but David refused. He would not allow his companion to touch the life of the man who was God's anointed.

It was with complete reliance upon God that David crept into the midst of this hostile force and took away the spear and water cruse from Saul's side. Then David and Abishai quietly made their way through the sleeping soldiers again and out of the camp without any man seeing it or being awake to know anything about it (v. 12).

Early the next morning David awakened Saul and his men by calling to them from a safe distance. "The wicked flee when no man pursueth: but the righteous are bold as a lion"

(Prov. 28:1), was true in David's experience. This took courage on his part but with the Lord ruling his heart no man could intimidate him. David reminds us of Paul before Agrippa and of more recent history in which Luther defied the church and secular leaders of his day, or John Knox who defied his queen as he stood for the truth of God. Someone has said, "If we tremble before worms of dust, it is because we do not tremble before God." David feared God so the fear of man was not in his heart.

When David called to Saul and Abner, Abner answered back: "Who art thou that criest to the king?" (v. 14). And David said to him "Art not thou a valiant man? and who is like to thee in Israel? wherefore then hast thou not kept thy lord the king? for there came one of the people in to destroy the king thy lord. This thing is not good that thou hast done. As the Lord liveth, ye are worthy to die, because ye have not kept your master, the Lord's anointed. And now see where the king's spear is, and the cruse of water that was at his bolster" (vv. 15,16). Abner was completely humiliated before his master Saul, and once more Saul is brought face to face with his insane jealousy and the wonderful restraint in the heart of David.

Saul then joined in the conversation saying, "Is this thy voice, my son David? And David said, It is my voice, my lord, O king. And he said, Wherefore doth my lord thus pursue after his servant? for what have I done? or what evil is in mine hand?" (vv. 17,18).

David went on to remind Saul that he had driven David out from God's inheritance and that was just as good as saying that he should serve other gods. He was not allowed to come near the Tabernacle and was hunted like a flea or a partridge. Then Saul admitted, "I have sinned, I have played the fool, and have erred exceedingly." David asked Saul to send someone up to get the spear and the cruse, for David wanted to prove to Saul that he had nothing against him. In verse 24 David said, "And, behold, as thy life was much set by this day in mine eyes, so let my life be much set by in the eyes of the Lord, and let him deliver me out of all tribulation." What he was saying was that he had held the life of Saul precious when he could easily have taken it. But David committed his life to the Lord and he did not say to Saul, "You hold my life precious." Instead he stated that the Lord would hold his life precious and the Lord would deliver him out of tribulation. David put no confidence in man, only in God. It is true that a man of God is to be trusted in certain respects, but not in the sense that we would put trust in a man as we put trust in God. Even the best of men are still men.

It was following this that David and Saul exchanged words for the last time on earth. Saul said to David, "Blessed be thou, my son David: thou shalt both do great things, and also shalt still prevail. So David went on his way, and Saul returned to his place" (v. 25). In another passage we are told that Saul "sought him no more." Yet, David hid from Saul for four more years not being sure when the king might seek his life again. At the end of that time Saul died in battle.

David's Lapse of Faith, I Samuel 27

We will find that Satan's attacks on us are often heaviest right after we experience a great victory of faith. A good example of this is Elijah after he had defeated the prophets of Baal on Mount Carmel. He called down fire from heaven and also destroyed the leaders of that idolatrous system. Then he became afraid of Jezebel's threats and ran for his life.

After Joshua's great victory at Jericho, Israel suffered two sad defeats. One was at Ai and the other had to do with the Gibeonites who were able to deceive Joshua through a stratagem.

So David, after this encounter with Saul, began to sing, but his song was in a minor key. We find in the first verse of chapter 27 that David said in his heart, "I shall now perish one day by the hand of Saul: there is nothing better for me than that I should speedily escape into the land of the Philistines; and Saul shall despair of me, to seek me any more in any coast of Israel: so shall I escape out of his hand." Once again David's heart was not right with God in that he doubted Him. The enemy shot his dart and found an open place in David's armor. Because of that he made a wrong decision in leaving his own land. This can happen to any of us when we look at the victory instead of at the Lord who provides victory. However, let us remember that these experiences of David were met on his way to learning greater obedience. In spite of David's failures, God was gracious in His dealing with His servant as He is with all of us who really want to please Him.

Paul would not even look at past victories for victories in the future. He said, "Forgetting those things which are behind, and reaching forth unto those things which are before, I press toward the mark of the prize of the high calling of God in Christ Jesus" (Phil. 4:13,14). Our Christian life is not made up of mountain-top experiences one right after another. There are valleys in between, but these valleys need not be valleys of defeat though they are valleys of testing. It is only as we depend upon God that we can be victorious.

We cannot repeat to ourselves often enough such passages of Scripture as Luke 9:23: "If any man will come after me, let him deny himself, and take up his cross daily, and follow me." Then there is Galatians 2:20, another key verse with regard to the victorious pathway for the believer: "I am crucified with Christ: nevertheless I live; yet not I, but Christ liveth in me: and the life which I now live in the flesh I live by the faith of the Son of God, who loved me, and gave himself for me."

We must be constantly reminded of Peter's words when he wrote, "Be sober, be vigilant; because your adversary the devil, as a roaring lion, walketh about, seeking whom he may devour: Whom resist stedfast in the faith, knowing that the same afflictions are accomplished in your brethren that are in the world. But the God of all grace, who hath called us unto his eternal glory by Christ Jesus, after that ye have suffered a while, make you perfect, stablish, strengthen, settle you" (I Pet. 5:8-10).

God permits testing to come but we still must in faith resist Satan. David wrote some Psalms at this time which are very illuminating on this point. In Psalm 10:1 we find him saying, "Why standest thou afar off, O Lord? why hidest thou thyself in times of trouble?" Or in Psalm 13:1, another written at this time: "How long wilt thou forget me, O Lord? for ever? how long wilt thou hide thy face from me?" Then there is Psalm 22 which, of course, looks forward to a greater David but the cry was, "My God, my God, why hast thou forsaken me? why art thou so far from helping me, and from the words of my roaring?" These are all Psalms of David when he cried out in despair feeling as though God had forsaken him.

David was in very difficult circumstances, because Saul was constantly hounding him. David had 600 men with him and undoubtedly there were many families also that had to be provided for. How does one hide 600 men and their families? It is no wonder, from the human standpoint, why David said, "I shall now perish one of these days by the hand of Saul."

A committed Christian will always be a special target of Satan's onslaughts. One of the chief methods Satan will use on a committed Christian will be to cause doubt. It was through doubt that he caused Adam and Eve to sin. That which is not of faith, remember, is of sin. And the battle of the committed Christian is not a battle so much against flesh and blood, but against spiritual forces, against principalities and powers in heavenly places.

Satan's primary interest is not us, but the Lord who indwells us. It is His life in us that Satan wants to harm.

If this sounds strange to you who read this, and you have not experienced it in your own heart, your Christian experience is shallow. If you will fully commit yourself to the Lord, you will begin to realize the truth of these things we have seen in David's life. God allows various testings to come, but He promises to save us out of them all if we will but trust him. It is as we learn to trust Him in each succeeding test that we grow stronger in our Christian lives.

For the second time David fled to Israel's enemies thinking he would find a safe place among them. Apparently his reasoning was that if he went to the land of the Philistines, he would be safe from Saul because Saul was afraid of them. That sounded like good reasoning, but it was only human reasoning. It led David into difficulties that could have been avoided had his trust remained strong in the Lord. We read, however, that when David sent to Achish the King of Gath, Saul did not seek him any more.

Achish, at David's request, gave him Ziklag for a city to dwell in with his men and their families. He dwelt there a full year and four months. This may have seemed to David to be a victory, but in reality Satan had won a battle. The pressure of pursuit on David was released, but the peace he lived in was a false one.

Many of us are harrassed by different kinds of pressures. Some people even have periods of great depression and instead of turning to God turn to drugs. David may have felt that by moving into Philistine territory Satan had been removed from him. In reality David paid a very great price for what freedom and peace he thought was his. He moved into enemy territory and Satan "got off his neck" so to speak; but as long as David was out of the will of God, the victory belonged to Satan.

In a sense, by moving into enemy territory, David was a deserter in the eyes of his own people. He gave advantage to the greatest enemy who was Satan himself.

The city of Ziklag had once belonged to the tribe of Simeon. It had been given to them by Joshua, but they were very careless and did not drive out the enemy as they should. Simeon tried co-existence but it just did not work. It was for this reason that Ziklag fell back into the hands of the Philistines. This is why we are sometimes defeated in our Christian lives. We try to live peacefully with that which is sinful but it cannot be done. At other times some of us try to win people for the Lord by going along with them in the evil things they do. Yet it has been proved time and again that we cannot win the lost by such tactics. This was how the tribe of Simeon failed, and we must be careful or we will do likewise.

David had temporary rest in this place, but one does not keep 600 fighting men happy couped up in a city. So we learn that "David and his men went up, and invaded the Geshurites, and the Gezrites, and the Amalekites: for those nations were of old the inhabitants of the land, as thou goest to Shur, even unto the land of Egypt" (vv. 8,9). David smote those different peoples in their land and took away the sheep and the oxen and the asses and the camels and the clothing and then returned to Ziklag. In this way, David was not inactive and he was fulfilling God's instructions that had been given many years before to the Israelites to drive out the wicked and idolatrous people from Canaan.

His work was very thorough for we read: "He left not alive man nor woman, nor anything of that nature." The reason is not hard to find. When Achish asked David where he had been, David said, "Against the south of Judah, and against the south of the Jerahmeelites, and against the south of the Kenites" (v. 10). This was deceptive. It was not true. But by destroying all persons in those areas that David invaded, there was no one left to bring news to Achish concerning what David had done. In fact, Achish thought David would be so abhorred by his own people that he would be a servant to the king of Gath forever.

Remember, all of this started with doubt. David had not yet learned what a serious thing it is to doubt God and His faithfulness. David did not dare tell Achish that he had been out against these enemies of Israel, for these enemies of Israel were the friends of the Philistines. He hid his true actions behind lies. He found, however, that he had exchanged the promises of the God of truth for the laws of Ziklag, and they were not adequate at all.

David had acted in panic when he had said in his heart that there was no hope for his safety while he stayed in Judah. This is something all of us need to be aware of. We should never act in panic. When troubles strike, let us carry them to God and let Him bring peace and quiet of heart to us. We cannot quiet ourselves but we can be quieted in God's presence. His mercy is for us at any time. The door to His throne of grace is ever open. He has promised never to leave us nor forsake us. We will always regret it if we act in panic. This was what made the Israelites want Moses to send them back to Egypt just shortly after they had been delivered from bondage. Moses, however, with his quiet confidence in the Lord led them safely to the Red Sea and safely through it also.

We, too, must remember to wait upon the Lord and have confidence in Him. God's promises are sure, but they are also conditional on the fact that we will act in righteousness. David, when he acted in deceit, forfeited the promises of God for the time being.

God permitted David to get into these difficulties though it was not necessary for David to have gone in this direction. God, of course, being sovereign could have stopped David, but it was necessary apparently for David to learn these lessons "the hard way." And the Lord is always gracious to those who are of a broken heart and saves such as are of a contrite spirit. In other words, when we accept the correction that God sends, then He can work once more to fulfil His will in our hearts and lives.

CHAPTER TEN

RETURN TO SPIRITUAL SANITY

I Samuel 28, 29, 30

We have seen how David through doubting God and then through deceit and lies had worked himself into a very serious situation. As we look at these next chapters, however, we will see his return to spiritual sanity. This was brought about through true repentance on his part. Although David had his spiritual lapses, he also had his great victories and returned in great strength to the will and purposes of God.

The way out of those difficulties was not easy. David and his men became the bodyguard to Achish, king of Gath, and this soon put David in a sore dilemma. The Philistines decided to go against the Israelites and David apparently could see no way out of going along and fighting against his own people. He had a weakness for telling lies when doubts came into his heart. This was one of his besetting sins. He had lied to Jonathan and through Jonathan to Saul. He had lied to Ahimelech and that had brought death to 85 priests.

David was aware of this tendency and in Psalm 119:29 uttered this prayer: "Remove from me the way of lying." Indeed, it was only God who could deliver him from this recurring sin. If he were to go to Achish and tell him what he had really been doing in that year and four months, he would immediately have been in the king's disfavor. When a rock starts rolling downhill, it gains momentum. This is what David found with regard to his lies. It was not God who had brought David to this place but his own desires, for we read in James 1:14,15: "But every man is tempted, when he is drawn away of his own lusts, and enticed. Then when lust hath conceived, it bringeth forth sin: and sin, when it is finished, bringeth forth death."

One wrong step leads to another. A young woman who goes out with a young man of questionable character makes a serious mistake. Soon, she may have to withstand advances, or she may succumb in the end to sin. Christians have been drawn into this kind of thing by dating an unsaved person thinking there is no harm in it. But one thing leads to another and before long what started out as a seemingly friendly companionship, ends in moral and spiritual disaster.

We can see also from David's case that when a Christian turns to the world for help, he can expect the world to ask him to pay for it. This is the very dilemma that David found himself in as bodyguard to Achish. If David followed Achish into battle against Israel, David would forfeit his right to be king of Israel. If he told Achish that he would not go with him to battle against Israel, then he would lose his haven of protection in Gath and might be fortunate to escape with his life.

The saving factor in David's case was that he was a man responsive to the dealing of God even though his faith lapsed at times. He had a tender conscience which God knew how to reach. God could have let him suffer this out, for surely David had it coming to him. Thank God His ways are not our ways and His thoughts are not our thoughts! There is mercy with the Lord.

We learn from the 12th chapter of the Book of Hebrews that God deals with us as with sons. Moreover, there is a world of difference between the sin of doubt on the part of David and the sin of rebellion and rejection on the part of Saul. David did not rebel in the sense that Saul did. He slipped into sin without willfully going against God. Saul, on the other hand, had so rejected the will of God for him that when he sought God's help he could not find it.

The story of Saul's visit to the witch of En-dor is well known. Samuel had been dead for some time, and Saul had no one he could turn to who would reveal to him God's will. It was in keeping with Saul's character to have issued orders to destroy all persons who sought contact with the dead such as the witch of En-dor and then, when he found himself facing a real difficulty, to seek the help of just such an evil person.

The witch of En-dor was terrified when she discovered that it was not the evil spirit for whom she was a medium who appeared to Saul. It was Samuel himself, and he said to the king: "For the Lord hath rent the kingdom out of thine hand, and given it to thy neighbour, even to David: Because thou obeyedst not the voice of the Lord, nor executedst his fierce wrath upon Amalek, therefore hath the Lord done this thing unto thee this day" (I Sam. 28:17,18).

Once again we see that Saul's great sin was the sin of rebellion against the will of God in refusing to destroy Amalek. Saul set his own will up against God's will. David was not rebellious in this respect.

Psalm 18 was written during a time just such as this that David was experiencing. Its verses help us understand something of the working of his heart. "I will call upon the Lord, who is worthy to be praised: so shall I be saved from mine enemies. The sorrows of death compassed me, and the floods of ungodly men made me afraid. The sorrows of hell compassed me about: the snares of death prevented me. In my distress I called upon the Lord, and cried unto my God." David also learned that the steps of a good man "are ordered by the Lord: and he delighteth in his way. Though he fall, he shall not be utterly cast down: for the Lord upholdeth him with his hand" (Ps. 37:23,24).

David found in all this experience that he was delivered from total disgrace through God's mercy but not from suffering.

The best of men have the same wicked nature. What counts with God is our attitude toward this sin nature. Paul says in Romans 7:18: "For I know that in me (that is, in my flesh,) dwelleth no good thing: for to will is present with me;

but how to perform that which is good I find not." Paul acknowledges that there is a desire in his heart to do good, but there is also sinfulness in his heart that he does not know how to control.

Jeremiah expresses the truth very clearly in the following words: "The heart is deceitful above all things, and desperately wicked: who can know it?" (17:9,10). Jeremiah is speaking here of the nature of the natural man. The heart he speaks of here is the same as what Paul calls the flesh, or the flesh nature in Romans 7. Jeremiah continues his subject by saying, "I the Lord search the heart, I try the reins [the affections of men], even to give every man according to his ways, and according to the fruit of his doings."

As far as David was concerned, he was a man after the heart of God, because he did want to do the will of God. He slipped and fell but arose again by the mercy of God. He had some hard lessons to learn, and like most of us he learned some of them the hard way. But it was in times like these that David called on the Lord for help; he knew by experience the truth of Psalm 34:18: "The Lord is nigh unto them that are of a broken heart; and saveth such as be of a contrite spirit."

We are all going to be tested and tried, but if we will remember the admonition Paul gives in Ephesians 6 that we wrestle not against flesh and blood, but against principalities and powers, then we will surely obey God. We will put on the whole armor of God that we might be able to stand in the evil day.

Just like David we have to be brought to the end of ourselves before we will look to the Lord for help. This was the case with Paul when he declared in Romans 7: "O wretched man that I am! who shall deliver me from the body of this death?" Paul found his deliverer in Christ.

It was failure to do this that was the secret of Saul's continued rebellion against God. He was willing to be straightened out with men but not with God. He did not at any time fully repent of his sin and turn from it. On the other hand, David not only turned from his sin but turned his whole life over to God again and again.

God never overlooks sin. At the same time He deals as a father with those of His children who fall into sin and disciplines them. For whom the Lord loves He chastens and scourges every son He receives. We also learn from the Scriptures: "The Lord preserveth all them that love him" (Ps. 145:20). "The Lord is faithful, who shall stablish you, and keep you from evil" (II Thess. 3:3). In the benediction at the end of his short letter, Jude writes: "Now unto him that is able to keep you from falling, and to present you faultless before the presence of his glory with exceeding joy" (v. 24). The Lord Jesus prayed for His disciples and taught them and us to pray: "Keep us from evil," literally "keep us from the evil one." The Lord Jesus intercedes for us as we learn from John 17:11,12: "And now I am no more in the world, but these are in the world, and I come to thee. Holy Father, keep through thine own name those whom thou hast given me, that they may be one, as we are. I have kept them, but now come I to thee." Keep them from what? From the snare of the fowler, the Evil One who tries to mar our spiritual lives.

If our hearts are right, God will always make a way of escape for us. This is the promise of I Corinthians 10:13: "There hath no temptation [testing] taken you but such as is common to man: but God is faithful, who will not suffer you to be tempted above that ye are able; but will with the temptation also make a way to escape, that ye may be able to bear it."

Now we can see how God works to deliver David from the dilemma sin had gotten him into in Gath. He must have been a troubled man when Achish told him that he and other Philistine princes were going up against Israel. But when those princes came, they were alarmed and indignant to find Hebrews in the army of Achish. They said, "What do these Hebrews here?" That was a good question and is a question the world has a right to ask when Christians are out of place.

Worldly people seem to know better than some of us who claim the name of Christ that we ought to have standards different from theirs.

The leaders of the other groups of Philistines would have nothing to do with David and his men and practically told Achish to leave him behind. They had good reason for this. They remembered what David had done to them years before. The Hebrew women had sung of David slaying his ten thousands, and Saul his thousands. They did not want a man on their side who had turned traitor to Israel. He might turn around again and betray the Philistines. Moreover, he might do that at a time when he could turn the battle against them. There is a saying that goes something like this: "If a man lies once, you won't believe him even if he tells the truth the next time." It looked to the Philistines as though David had betrayed his own people, though we know from the record that he had not gone against the Israelites at all. Nevertheless, the Philistines wanted nothing to do with him.

We often think that we must mix with the world in order to win the people of the world. We think that by compromising we will win them to the Lord. This is often an argument given by Christian young people who marry unbelievers. They feel that after they are married they will be able to win their mate to Christ. But it rarely works out that way. It is usually the other way around. Disaster often follows.

Even some churches have been letting down the bars in this respect and have incorporated worldly activities into their church life. They are careful, of course, to give these activities Christian names and to put them under Christian auspices. They think in this way they will win the lost. This was about the situation David found himself in, and for awhile it almost looked like the end of the line for him.

God in His mercy has His way of keeping a man from going completely to ruin. David was dismissed by Achish from the army and this dismissal was his way out. Achish was satisfied with him but the other princes of the Philistines were not. This was how God made it possible for David to escape from this great dilemma. It was God who kept David from falling into the greater tragedy of actually fighting against his own people.

The Lord taught me a lesson at the beginning of the work of this Broadcast in Nebraska for which I have always thanked Him. Back in 1939 when I came to Lincoln for the first time I did not know anyone, but I had been given the name of a fine Christian man who had a good deal of this world's goods, and was using it for the Lord. I was told that if I would ask this man, he would possibly help me get the Broadcast started. He did not believe he should and turned down my request.

Years later, when the Broadcast had considerably increased in its outreach, this good brother came to me more than once in tears almost apologizing for not having helped me get started. My reply was, "Brother, this was God's doings. This was God's way of removing any hope or any confidence in any man with regard to the support of this work. God had asked us to leave home and friends and an assured income to go to a place He would show us. I came and asked for your help, but it was not God's plan for me, and God saw to it that I did not fall into the mistake of placing my trust in man. He put me in such a position that I had to trust Him absolutely." Then I said to this brother, "God bless you; you did not know it, but you were in the will of God in turning me down."

God does not forsake the man after His own heart even though that man fails Him at times. Psalm 103 has searched my heart in this particular phase of Christian truth many times. There we read: "Like as a father pitieth his children, so the Lord pitieth them that fear him. For he knoweth our frame; he remembereth that we are dust" (vv. 13,14). There may be lapses of faith. His children may fall into the snares of the Devil, but God does not forsake us forever. He knows our frame and our weaknesses and nothing can separate us from the love of God.

Is it any wonder that Paul wrote in Romans 8:38: "For

I am persuaded, that neither death, nor life, nor angels, nor principalities, nor powers, nor things present, nor things to come, nor height, nor depth, nor any other creature, shall be able to separate us from the love of God, which is in Christ Jesus our Lord"? Because of His love, God may chastise us and may allow us to pass through some deep valleys, but He will be with us and lead us through.

God was watching over David in all his wanderings, even in the times when David had failed Him. It was in David's heart to do the will of God and those desires were awakened through the experiences he passed through. Ignorant of being instruments in God's hands, the Philistine lords worked out God's sovereign plan in David's restoration. God spared David from falling into greater disgrace and shame, but He did not overlook David's behavior. There were still some things David had to learn out of this whole series of incidents, and God is the Master Teacher.

The timing of David's dismissal from the Philistine army was perfect. While David marched in one direction the Amalekites were stirred up by God to invade the Philistine territory from the other direction. This brought David face to face with another great crisis in his life.

Ziklag, I Samuel 30

The town where David and his men were making their home was in the very southern part of the land of Canaan. It took him and his men three days to travel from the Philistine camp to their home city. On arrival they found "the Amalekites had invaded the south, and Ziklag, and smitten Ziklag, and burned it with fire; And had taken the women captives, that were therein: they slew not any, either great or small, but carried them away, and went on their way" (vv. 1,2). If you stop to think of it a moment, you will realize that had Saul carried out God's instructions there would have been no Amalekites left to carry on such a raid as they made on Ziklag. They were bitter enemies of Israel and apparently would never be satisfied with less than the extermination of

God's people. God is a merciful God and He had borne with their evil ways for many years until the cup of their iniquity was full. Not until then did God decree their end. When David and his men reached Ziklag, they found the city empty of its inhabitants and burned.

David could be a stubborn man, and then it took strong measures to bring His will into line with the will of God again. This was a heart-breaking experience for David to pass through, but apparently it was needed to bring him to complete restoration to the will of God.

We cannot help but contrast the difference between the conduct of David when he invaded the country of the Amalekites and their conduct when they raided Ziklag. David left neither man nor woman alive in the particular areas he invaded and he took away all the sheep, oxen, asses and camels. There was no one to carry the message to Achish that David had been spoiling peoples friendly to the Philistines. When the Amalekites invaded David's home city, they took everybody alive and, of course, they took all the spoil. It was through God's permission the Amalekites descended on Ziklag, and God used them to correct David but not to destroy him. The sovereign plan of God for David's life was still in effect. This experience was designed to fulfil God's plan in his life. We, too, should recognize that God has a sovereign plan for each of us. We should find out what it is and stay in the will of God and be willing instruments in His hands. This does not mean we will not have perplexities and difficulties, but it will mean that we will not have regrets and heartaches because of disobedience.

When David and his men found Ziklag burned with fire and their wives and their children gone, they wept. This was a bitter blow to all of them. David in particular, however, tasted the bitterness of being without God's protection. He had been miraculously taken care of on many other occasions but now that protection had been removed for the time being. David had exchanged the king of Gath and a walled city for the Spirit of the Lord and found no protection in man. It is the Spirit of the Lord who encamps round about His people and protects them. How often we forget this.

In all ages men have been concerned with security, particularly material and economic security. Yet one of these days we will find out that these things mean nothing if God is not in them. It is His presence and fellowship that are the essentials in life.

It is noteworthy that the Lord mentions very particularly "David's two wives were taken captives, Ahinoam the Jezreelitess, and Abigail the wife of Nabal the Carmelite." Why does God bring this matter up again? The reason is, I believe, that these were not lawfully David's wives. God made one man and one woman for each other, and David stepped out of the will of God in this area. True, others were doing it, but that was no excuse for David who was God's man. Now, for a time at least, they were lost of him. God is surely showing something here of His displeasure with polygamy, a form of marriage that has been practiced in one way or another since early times and has even been a fruitful source of trouble in families and nations.

David was in great distress, and no wonder: "The people spake of stoning him, because the soul of all the people was grieved, every man for his sons and for his daughters: but David encouraged himself in the Lord his God." Up to this point a great deal of David's problems had arisen with men or groups outside his own immediate army. Now revolt is seemingly on the way. His own trusted men became mutinous when they discovered their great loss. David was made to drink a cup here that he had never tasted before. It helped bring him completely to the end of himself. He was left alone, none of his men stood with him—but God."

Sometimes being a leader can be a very lonely job. Someone sent me this—"A leader is a lonely man. He follows visions that others cannot see. He moves ahead when others lag behind. He walks in solitude with God driven on by a burning desire to achieve goals that to others seem visionary and impractical, because leaders are non-conformists. They are looked upon with some suspicion by the run of the mill of the crowd. Men who lead are certain targets for the biting barbs of criticism. Their fearless, clear, compelling manner makes them a prey to those who do not understand them. But the church needs leaders today, men who will bear criticism and reproach for the cause of Christ; men who will stand up when others fail and fall, who will go on when others faint. Who will be a leader today?"

Such a leader was David, but he was now brought to the end of himself. This reminds us of the experience of Jacob who the night before he met Esau and would have to make matters right with him, sent all his family and his servants from him and remained behind and there wrestled a man with him. David in this experience touched rock bottom, then he reached up for God. This was the turning point at this time in his life.

These matters were all perfectly timed by God. Had David been a week later in arriving, the pursuit of the Amalekites might have been hopeless, and the consequences to David would have been greater. But everything is timed by God in our lives. Everything has a season the Word tells us. "My times are in thy hands" we read in God's Word. In Job 14 we find Job saying, "Seeing his days are determined, the number of his months are with thee, thou hast appointed his bounds and he cannot pass. If a man die, shall he live again? all the days of my appointed time will I wait, till my change come." There Job speaks of "my appointed time." In Job 7:1 we find these words: "Is there not an appointed time to man upon earth? are not his days also like the days of the hireling?" In other words, are not man's days on earth somewhat like that of a man who is employed by another? The times are set and the duties set. Just so with man for whom God sets the appointed times.

In God's hand "is the soul of every living thing, and the breath of all mankind" (Job 12:10). The Psalmist brings in this same truth when he prays: "Lord, make me to know mine end, and the measure of my days, what it is; that I may know how frail I am" (Ps. 39:4). Life is not an accident and the events of life are not accidents. God controls the measure of our days and the timing of the events of our days also.

No one of us has assurance of time beyond the moment we are now living. Our time may be up today, it might be tomorrow. If you are not a believer in Christ, why not receive him as your Saviour now? Now is the accepted time. Now is the day of salvation. If you have intended to surrender, why not do it now? Your time may be up tomorrow also. Remember, God said to one man "Thou fool, this night thy soul shall be required of thee: then whose shall those things be, which thou hast provided?"

David, as we have said, was brought to the end of himself. What would be our reaction if all our possessions were taken away, our loved ones likewise, and then our friends turn against us? Could we stand it? This has happened to more than one believer. Listen to what the Psalmist says in Psalm 55:12: "For it was not an enemy that reproached me; then I could have borne it: neither was it he that hated me that did magnify himself against me; then I would have hid myself from him [this is exactly what David had done for eight years having Saul as his enemy]: But it was thou, a man mine equal, my guide, and mine acquaintance. We took sweet counsel together, and walked unto the house of God in company." Then David adds, "As for me, I will call upon God; and the Lord shall save me." These were the words he spoke when he came to the end of himself. David found his only source of comfort in the Lord. This was why he encouraged himself in the Lord.

It was with a contrite heart that David turned to the Lord. This was why he could write: "The righteous cry, and the Lord heareth, and delivereth them out of all their troubles. The Lord is nigh unto them that are of a broken heart; and saveth such as be of a contrite spirit. Many are the afflictions of the righteous: but the Lord delivereth him out of them all." Isaiah tells us in his prophecy: "For thus saith the high and lofty One that inhabiteth eternity, whose name is Holy; I dwell in the high and holy place, with him also that is of a contrite and humble spirit, to revive the spirit of the humble, and to revive the heart of the contrite ones" (57:15). In chapter 66 Isaiah says: "But to this man will I look, even to him that is poor and of a contrite spirit, and trembleth at my word."

The word "contrite" means broken or crushed under the weight of conscious guilt. The two words are brought together in Psalm 34 where it speaks of "a broken and a contrite spirit." Putting these two words "broken" and "contrite" together constitute an intensity of expression. There are too many dry-eyed Christians in repentance. There are not enough who show brokenheartedness.

God does not reveal to us in this section just all that went on between Him and David. Some of those things belong in the secret places; but God does not leave us without knowledge of what is involved in this matter of brokenheartedness. Before there can be comfort and consolation, there must be conviction, contrition, confession and repentance. A man who covers his sins will not prosper, but the one who confesses and forsakes them will find mercy (Prov. 28:13).

Nothing Between

Nothing between my soul and the Saviour,
Naught of this world's delusive dream;
I have renounced all sinful pleasure,
Jesus is mine; let nothing between.

Nothing between like worldly pleasure;
Habits of life, though harmless they seem,
Must not my heart from Him ever sever—
He is my all, let nothing between.

Nothing between, e'en many hard trials,
Though the whole world against me convene;
Watching with prayer and much self-denial,
I'll triumph at last, with nothing between.

Nothing between my soul and the Saviour,
So that His blessed face may be seen;
Nothing preventing the least of His favor,
Keep the way clear! Let nothing between.

The first thing David did after encouraging himself in the Lord, was to ask Abiathar the priest to bring the ephod. When it was brought, David inquired of the Lord saying, "Shall I pursue after this troop? shall I overtake them? And he [God] answered him, Pursue: for thou shalt surely overtake them, and without fail recover all. So David went, he and the six hundred men that were with him" (vv. 8,9). The action was not long in following once David knew God's mind.

Some of us might be inclined to think that the normal thing would have been for David to start out after the Amalekites without even asking the Lord about it. We might think this was the obvious thing to do. But remember, David had had enough of his own reasoning. He had followed his own reasoning in going to Gath and by it had escaped from the hand of Saul, but he got himself into more difficulties than he ever expected. The seemingly natural thing to do may not always be the right thing so far as God is concerned. When David's fellowship was restored with the Lord, David let the Lord guide his steps.

God's Word admonishes us: "Trust in the Lord with all thine heart; and lean not unto thine own understanding" (Prov. 3:5). This was not written at the time David was living, but David through experience found the truth of this. It was David's son who wrote this verse and added: "In all thy ways acknowledge him, and he shall direct thy paths. Be not wise in thine own eyes: but fear the Lord, and depart from evil." This then was why David who had the truth of these things in his heart, first asked the Lord if he should go, and if he went, would he be able to overtake the enemy. God reassured him, telling him he should go and that he would overtake the enemy, and would recover all the captives and the spoil.

There was another blessing to David along with his

obedience in following God's orders at this point. David's men had been angry with him feeling that it was David's fault they had lost their families and their possessions. If David had been in touch with the Lord all the time they followed him, they would not have experienced these harsh results. They felt they were being punished for David's wrongdoings. But this was now changed. Without a doubt David told the men the result of his consulting of God, and they willingly followed him as their leader.

When David's lapse of faith took place, he lost his vision of God's caring for him. The vision of the believer should always be upward toward God and not visionary with presumptuous plans of what we will do. David having lost his vision of God's care thought he would perish. He failed to see that God is sovereign and that it is God who works in us both to will and to do of His good pleasure. The fact that David was anointed was God's assurance that David would be king. Because of the long wait until the fulfillment of that promise, David had allowed discouragement and doubt to enter his heart.

David had also lost his inward hunger and desire for the Lord. We read in Matthew 5:6: "Blessed are they which do hunger and thirst after righteousness: for they shall be filled." David had consulted his own heart instead of going to God to find out what His mind was concerning His servant's life. Having failed to pray or inquire of the Lord, David had lost his spiritual thirst for the things of God.

In the third place, because David had lost his vision and his spiritual thirst, he had also lost that communion that allows the Holy Spirit to govern the believer's actions. These actions governed by the Spirit are the result of a correct vision and desire in the heart. Vision is the outward look toward heaven, for we learn that where there is no vision the people perish. Passion is that inward desire, the inward hunger and compassion of the soul for the will of God. The action that is controlled by the Holy Spirit is released as the result of correct vision and passion under the will of God.

David lost his vision because he had forgotten God's promises. He came to the place where he did not believe God had the power or the ability to protect him. But let us learn from David that it is more important that we believe what God has said to us in the Scriptures than that we can always understand it or explain it. There is a vast difference between knowing the God of the Word and knowing the Word of God. Many people know a lot about what the Word of God says, but it is of more importance to know the God of the Word. We come to know the God of the Word as we obey what we know of the Word of God.

An illustration of this is given in the Book of Isaiah. We learn that Isaiah "saw the Lord sitting upon a throne, high and lifted up." He also saw angelic beings saying to one another "Holy, holy, holy, is the Lord of hosts." We learn also that "the posts of the door moved at the voice of him that cried, and the house was filled with smoke." It was then that Isaiah cried, "Woe is me! for I am undone; because I am a man of unclean lips, and I dwell in the midst of people of unclean lips: for mine eyes have seen the King, the Lord of hosts. Then flew one of the seraphims unto me, having a live coal in his hand, which he had taken with the tongs from off the altar: And he laid it upon my mouth, and said, Lo, this hath touched thy lips; and thine iniquity is taken away, and thy sin purged. Also I heard the voice of the Lord, saying, Whom shall I send, and who will go for us? Then said I, Here am I; send me. And he said, Go, and tell this people."

An examination of this Scripture shows us that Isaiah first had a vision of God's holiness and this brought about a consciousness of his own sinfulness and depravity. This in turn lead to an inward cleansing as the coal was brought from the altar to him. Following this was the vision of the helplessness of the people who were without God. The end result was a commission to Isaiah to go with God's message. Isaiah's vision of God's holiness brought about confession. His vision of his own sinfulness brought about cleansing. His vision of the hopelessness of the people without God brought about a heavenly commission. Isaiah had a vision. He saw God.

Have we had such a vision, a vision that comes through the Word of God and through the Holy Spirit? Where is our passion? Where is our action as the result of our vision and passion? The man who sins stops praying, and I fear that is what happened to David. But the man who begins to pray, stops sinning and that is an important lesson for us to learn.

Let us remember also that the person who gossips about another will never really pray for him. But the man who prays for another will not gossip about him. When David had his vision and his passion restored, his actions lined up with the will of God. He recovered all of the families and all of the property; best of all, he recovered his spiritual fellowship and became useful again in the plans of God.

So far as circumstances are concerned, David had little to go on at first to show he was in the will of God. He started out from Ziklag in obedience to God's promises. Then when he and his men came to the brook Besor, 200 of his soldiers were so weak that they could not continue the journey. They had to be left behind while David pushed on with only 400 men. Had he been looking only at the circumstances, David might have lost heart.

As they followed along after the Amalekites they found an Egyptian slave who, because of illness, had been left behind by his Amalekite master. For three days and nights he had had nothing to eat or drink and when found appeared about ready to die. David's men fed him and gave him water to drink and his strength returned. They persuaded him to guide them to where the Amalekites were gathered. In this way David was able to make a surprise attack upon his enemies who were so delirious over their easy victory that they had become careless. The finding of this young Egyptian was one of the first circumstances that showed the hand of God in this venture.

The next has already been indicated in that the Amalekites became careless and spread out their forces and began to celebrate their victories. They were not in a compact group but scattered in small groups over a large area, eating and drinking and dancing, hardly in condition to put up strong resistance to their pursuers.

They were an easy prey to David and his men. Even though his group had been cut down by 200, David was able to route the enemy, only 400 young men escaping on camels.

Thus, "David rescued his two wives. And there was nothing lacking to them, neither small nor great, neither sons nor daughters, neither spoil, nor any thing that they had taken to them: David recovered all."

In addition to rescuing his own people and their possessions, David also captured the goods the Amalekites had stolen from the Philistines and the tribe of Judah.

When David and his victorious group reached the 200 who had to be left behind at the brook, some of his men proposed that they give back the wives and the children and the goods belonging to these 200, but not to share with them the other spoils. Their argument was that since they had not gone to war with the 400, they had no right to share in the spoils. David reversed this, however. He said, "For who will hearken unto you in this matter? but as his part is that goeth down to the battle, so shall his part be that tarrieth by the stuff: they shall part alike" (v. 24). This was a statute that David inaugurated then and established in Israel. It is a principle that is of great encouragement to us in the spiritual realm.

Very few of God's people have a public ministry, and very few of those who have such a ministry have a large one. A work such as Back to the Bible Broadcast is able to reach millions of people every day through the preaching of the Word and through the music in song. Those of you who listen to the program may feel that you cannot share in the reward of a ministry of this nature. But you can, if you are one who stays with the stuff. You can be one who is behind the scenes and makes this work possible through your prayers and gifts. God will not forget any who have had a part in carrying out His work whether this one or another.

The principle followed by David is as we have said a spiritual principle that God gave him. He was simply following the leading of the Holy Spirit in his life when he said there must be a proper division of the spoils. Every man was to share alike. This was not only a rule to be followed by soldiers in Israel, but it is a spiritual program that God follows according to many New Testament passages.

David's consideration went farther than just the men and families who had been with him through the years. Had it not been for the friends in Judah who had kept him and his men supplied with food, David would not have been able to do what he did. These friends believed that David would one day be king; consequently, their faith was also being tested over these years. They had also lost heavily in the invasion by the Amalekites, so when David shared with them the spoils of battle, he was only repaying kindnesses they had shown him and returning some of their possessions stolen by the Amalekites.

David's Return to His Land, II Samuel 1-3

About the time David returned to the land of Judah, the Philistines made war on Saul. The Israelites did not become subject to the Philistines then, at least not in any large numbers, but they did lose the battle. Saul and his son, Jonathan, and many of the other leaders in Israel were killed.

The Second Book of Samuel opens with the account of a messenger coming to David and telling him that Saul and Jonathan and many others were dead. Thinking to gain David's approval and possibly receive a reward from him, this messenger who was an Amalekite told David that it was at his hands Saul had died. He said he had come upon Saul who was still alive even after falling on his own sword. Saul had pleaded with him to kill him before the Philistines came upon him and mutilated his body while he was still alive. The young man claimed he did as Saul requested. Some Bible students believe the young man told the truth, others believe he lied, but whatever the correct version is, he took his story to the wrong man.

David had always had a strong aversion to raising his hand against God's anointed. Neither would he permit any of his own men to do it. So when this young Amalekite claimed to have killed Saul, David had him put to death.

What would be David's next move? Saul was dead and Jonathan, Saul's oldest son was dead, and since God had promised the kingdom to David, would this not be the right time for him to claim the throne? Everything was now in his favor, seemingly, but David was in no hurry. He made no fast move at this time. The circumstances seemed to be right for him, but David was learning to be careful of circumstances. They should be the last, not the first consideration in doing the will of God.

David trusted in the Lord with all his heart and did not lean to his own understanding in this situation. He was not wise in his own eyes but feared the Lord and departed from evil. David did not want what the Lord did not give to him. He would not take by force what God had promised but left it to the Lord to bring him to the throne in His own time.

So many of us make the mistake of feeling we have to help God fulfil His promises. There are times when this may be true, but we want to be sure it is God who is directing us. When something is grabbed quickly by us lest someone else take it, it is doubtful if we are following the Lord. No one can really take away from us that God has planned for us.

I have believed with all my heart from the day that God called us here to Back to the Bible Broadcast over a quarter of a century ago, that the Lord had already appointed the places and the persons from whom the support for this work was to come. There have been delays along the way and that is because some of God's people have not listened; but we seek to do as David did and keep our eyes on the Lord and not on men.

The second chapter of II Samuel opens with these words: "And it came to pass after this, that David enquired of the Lord, saying, Shall I go up into any of the cities of Judah? And the Lord said unto him, Go up. And David said, Whither shall I go up? And he said, Unto Hebron." David found and we, too, will find that we never lose anything by believing God and then patiently waiting upon Him. But we will surely suffer if we take things into our own hands and rush blindly ahead.

The word "Hebron" means "alliance" or "communion" which is a contrast to Ziklag which has reference to "self-will." Being allied with God and being in communion with Him, David was in a place to be led on in the will of God.

What do we as individuals know about our God? Is our fellowship complete with Him? Do we take such verses as II Corinthians 3:5 seriously? "Not that we are sufficient of ourselves to think any thing as of ourselves; but our sufficiency is of God." Or consider Colossians 2:9,10: "For in him dwelleth all the fulness of the Godhead bodily. And ye are complete in him."

David's men were not forgotten when he moved to Hebron. They went with him and took their households along. They had shared in his tribulations; now they were sharing in the blessings of his communion. Then we learn that the men of Judah came "And there they anointed David king over the house of Judah. And they told David, saying, That the men of Jabesh-gilead were they that buried Saul."

Here a bridgehead to the kingdom of Israel is established. David's reign began by reigning first over Judah. It was not necessary for David to take the throne; God saw that he received it. God moved him back to Hebron and his own tribe anointed him king.

Seven and a half years go by, however, before the whole kingdom is put under his hand. David still had to wait, but it was God's time he was waiting for, not man's.

While David was being made king over Judah, "Abner the son of Ner, captain of Saul's host, took Ish-bosheth the son of Saul, and brought him over to Mahanaim; And made him king over Gilead, and over the Ashurites, and over Jezreel, and over Ephraim, and over Benjamin, and over all Israel. Ish-bosheth Saul's son was forty years old when he began to reign over Israel, and reigned two years. But the house of Judah followed David. And the time that David was king in Hebron over the house of Judah was seven years and six months" (II Sam. 2:8-11).

We might wonder if David had made a mistake in not forcing the issue at once since it seemed to him that the major part of the kingdom had been lost. But David waited on God and wanted only what God gave him.

This matter of waiting on God, as we have seen before, is not necessarily just a matter of time. The element of discernment is involved. We must learn to distinguish the still small voice of God from the other voices that surround us from day to day. This is a day of confusion and many Christians are confused. They wonder if it is God who is speaking through some of the things they hear.

David pondered these things, thinking back over the eight years that he had to spend fleeing from Saul, then seven and a half more years in Hebron waiting God's time. Often he had to fight for his very life because of the efforts of Saul's supporters to overthrow David and establish one of Saul's descendants on the throne of all Israel.

David could say after looking back over this experience: "Fret not thyself because of evildoers, neither be thou envious against the workers of iniquity. For they shall soon be cut down like the grass, and wither as the green herb. Trust in the Lord, and do good; so shalt thou dwell in the land, and verily thou shalt be fed. Delight thyself also in the Lord; and he shall give thee the desires of thine heart. Commit thy way unto the Lord; trust also in him; and he shall bring it to pass" (Ps. 37). It may have seemed for awhile that Saul's son who was on the throne of the eleven tribes of Israel was prospering in his way, but David learned not to fret "because of him who prospereth in the way, because of the man who bringeth wicked devices to pass." He knew that those who waited upon the Lord would inherit the earth.

In fact, the wicked had no chance in plotting against the just and gnashing against him with their teeth because "The

Lord shall laugh at him: for he seeth that his day is coming."

Beginning with verse 32 of Psalm 37 we read: "The wicked watcheth the righteous, and seeketh to slay him. The Lord will not leave him in his hand, nor condemn him when he is judged. Wait on the Lord, and keep his way, and he shall exalt thee to inherit the land: when the wicked are cut off, thou shalt see it. I have seen the wicked in great power, and spreading himself like a green bay tree. Yet he passed away, and, lo, he was not: yea, I sought him, but he could not be found. Mark the perfect [mature] man, and behold the upright: for the end of that man is peace." Does it pay to wait on God? What we have learned about David tells us "Yes!"

The Rock That Is Higher Than I

O sometimes the shadows are deep,
And rough seems the path to the goal,
And sorrows, sometimes how they sweep
Like tempests down over the soul!

O sometimes how long seems the day,
And sometimes how weary my feet;
But toiling in life's dusty way,
The Rock's blessed shadow, how sweet!

O near to the Rock let me keep,
If blessings or sorrows prevail;
Or climbing the mountain way steep,
Or walking the shadowy vale.

O then to the Rock let me fly,
To the Rock that is higher than I!

CHAPTER ELEVEN

CORONATION DAY

II Samuel 3:17-21

David's waiting on the Lord indeed paid off. At the end of seven and a half years God began to move events to where David was finally crowned king of all Israel. Abner, who was general of the armies of Israel, had put Ish-bosheth on the throne of Saul to reign over eleven tribes. However, when Ish-bosheth quarreled with him concerning one of Saul's concubines, Abner retaliated by scheming to turn the kingdom over to David.

"And Abner had communication with the elders of Israel, saying, Ye sought for David in times past to be king over you . . . And Abner said unto David, I will arise and go, and will gather all Israel, unto my Lord the king [David], that they make a league with thee, and that thou mayest reign over all that thine heart desireth. And David sent Abner away; and he went in peace" (II Sam. 3:17-21).

A very practical admonition comes from a statement made by Abner. It is a word we can apply to our own hearts. Abner went to the people of Israel and said that they had sought for David in time past to be their king, and he added, "Now then do it" (v. 18). Make Christ King in your life. He is God's appointed King as David was appointed and then anointed for the kingship of Israel. Remember the name "Christ" means the "anointed of God" and as such He has been appointed and anointed to be King in our lives. So make Him King today.

The work of redemption that Christ has wrought for us

is a finished work. The work of the Holy Spirit, on the other hand, which is forming Christ in us, is progressive. Have we ever progressed beyond Calvary?

This is the burden of Hebrews 6:1 where we read: "Therefore leaving the principles of the doctrine of Christ, let us go on unto perfection [maturity]." Have we progressed beyond this stage of spiritual infancy? Do we know the difference between our position in Christ which is by faith and is forever settled in heaven, and our condition, our behavior among men? Having been born again we are children of God and are accepted before God in Jesus Christ. Our names are written in the Lamb's Book of Life and we have the assurance of an eternal home in heaven.

But there is another side of our lives as Christians. We live in this world before men, and though our behavior does not affect our new birth, our new birth makes a great difference in our behavior. The fact that we have trusted in Christ and are born into God's family is not changed by our behavior. On the other hand, the fact that we have been born into God's family is bound to eventually make a change in our behavior. We have been born again, "created in Christ Jesus unto good works." There will be a change in our behavior once we are born of God. Peter tells us that according to God's divine power He "hath given unto us all things that pertain unto life and godliness . . . Whereby are given unto us exceeding great and precious promises: that by these ye might be partakers of the divine nature, having escaped the corruption that is in the world through lust" (II Pet. 1:3,4).

There is no time like the present to make the Lord Jesus King in our lives. If we have allowed things to stand in the way, let us make this His coronation day in our hearts now.

Like David who never forced his kingship, Christ never forces His rulership over us. We have been made children of God through faith in Christ and Christ gives us His life. He is now waiting on us to offer ourselves to Him so that He might reign as King within. He takes what is offered Him. We must invite Him to come in and occupy the throne of our hearts.

I am afraid that some believers have offered Christ nothing at all even though they have taken of His salvation. Others may have offered Him "Hebron" which speaks of "communion" or "fellowship" with Him, but they have offered no more lest it interfere with their personal plans for their lives. Let us take Abner's suggestion and "do it." Make Christ King!

It is lack of making Christ King in the hearts that causes the civil war to rage within us. We have no peace. We hold on to the tottering kingdom of self and it cannot stand. But this is a costly war that benefits none but the Devil. While David was held off from becoming king of all Israel, there was nothing but civil war. As long as we keep Jesus Christ from ruling within, we will find ourselves without peace of heart. The Holy Spirit is waiting to take control and to settle that constant fight between the flesh and the Spirit. Why not give up? Why not turn over everything to the Lord? How long will we struggle to have our own way? Let us turn our lives over to Him now.

While the civil war raged in Israel, David became stronger and the family of Saul became weaker. But the kingdom was still divided. The self-life is the losing side. As long as it has any place in our lives we will face nothing but defeats, heartaches, losses and troubles. Perhaps we have met others who have made Christ their King. We see them victorious and joyful. They are not without their tribulations and trials, but these do not get them down. The longer we hold out on our Saviour, the more danger there is of hardening our hearts against Him. This is what Saul did. He was obedient for a time, but later on he neglected God, hardened his heart against the will of God, and so was rejected as king.

Remember that there is a very serious warning given to us in Hebrews 6: "For it is impossible for those who were once enlightened, and have tasted of the heavenly gift, and were made partakers of the Holy Ghost, And have tasted the good word of God, and the powers of the world to come, If they shall fall away, to renew them again unto repentance;

seeing they crucify to themselves the Son of God afresh, and put him to an open shame" (vv. 4-6). This all speaks of a man who has received salvation but has not gone on to yield himself completely to the Lord. It is not a question of losing salvation but of rejecting Christ's kingship and losing the blessings that go with it.

Elijah put a proposition to the children of Israel one day saying to them: "How long halt ye between two opinions? If the Lord be God, follow him, and if Baal, then follow him. The people answered him not a word." Let us answer God and say, "Yes" to Christ.

As long as David was only king of Judah but not all Israel, God's people could not have rest from their enemies round about. The Lord said of David, "By the hand of my servant David I will save my people Israel out of the hand of the Philistines, and out of the hand of all their enemies." Jesus must be King or He cannot save you in the way God plans. Almost without exception when the word "Jesus" is used or the word "Saviour," the word "Lord" is somewhere in the context. We cannot be saved from sin without giving up sin and turning from it. Our salvation consists of turning our lives over to him not only for forgiveness but also for His Lordship. If we want to be victorious Christians, we must let Him rule. We are reconciled to God by Christ's death, but we are saved from the power of sin by Christ's life (Rom. 5:10).

As long as David and Ish-bosheth both ruled over the tribes of Israel, there was neither peace nor safety. We, too, must choose between Christ and the self-life. Some day every knee will bow and acknowledge Christ as King according to Philippians 2:9-11 but not all knees will bow at that time voluntarily. We have that choice now. Let us do it gladly and do it right away.

Be Ye Strong in the Lord

"Be ye strong in the Lord, and the power of His might,"
Firmly standing for the truth of His word;
He shall lead you safely thro' the thickest of the fight,
You shall conquer in the name of the Lord.

"Be ye strong in the Lord, and the power of His might,"
For His promises shall never, never fail;
By thy right hand He'll hold thee while battling for the right,
Trusting Him thou shalt forever prevail.

Firmly stand for the right,
On to vict'ry at the King's command:
For the honor of the Lord, and the triumph of His word,
In the strength of the Lord firmly stand.

CHAPTER TWELVE

JERUSALEM MADE CENTER OF GOVERNMENT AND WORSHIP

II Samuel 5

Outstanding things began to take place as soon as David became king. In II Samuel 5 we read some of the events leading to the capture of Zion from the Jebusites. It was a very old city. We first read of it in the Bible in connection with Abraham who gave tithes to Melchizedek, God's priest and king of Salem. This was the city God had chosen to be the center of Israel's government and of God's habitation. It was almost four centuries after Joshua led the people into Canaan before the stronghold of Zion fell to the Israelites.

So impregnable did the Jebusites think their fortress to be that they jeered at David and his men, saying that the halt and the lame could hold it against David's army. "Nevertheless," we are told, "David took the strong hold of Zion: the same is the city of David" (II Sam. 5:7). David then moved into the city and made it the headquarters for his government, and later on it was to be made the central place of worship for God's people. This was "the place that he [God] hath chosen where his name shall be." Eventually Solomon's great temple was erected in Jerusalem. Best of all it will be from this city that the Lord Jesus Christ will rule in the Millennium and establish His New Jerusalem of which the Prophet Ezekiel speaks.

There is a rich lesson in spiritual truth for us here. There are habits of sin so deeply entrenched in our minds and bodies that we have struggled in vain against them from the day of our new birth. We may have felt it was no use to try to overcome these habits and that we might as well give up. What we need, of course, is to let the King, the Lord Jesus Christ, lead us in the battle against this entrenched sin. Just as the stronghold of the Jebusites which is typical of the power of sin in our lives, was overthrown; so will the power of sin in our life be broken and every area of it made to be under the control of our Lord and King. We can never route the enemy by ourselves. It must always be done through the strength of Christ.

The powers of Satan are great but the power of Christ is greater. We learn in Hebrews 2:14: "Forasmuch then as the children are partakers of flesh and blood, he also himself likewise took part of the same; that through death he might destroy him that had the power of death, that is, the devil; And deliver them who through fear of death were all their lifetime subject to bondage." Our Lord himself said in John 12:31,32: "Now is the judgment of this world: now shall the prince of this world be cast out. And I, if I be lifted up from the earth, will draw all men unto me." This, of course, spoke of Calvary but the truth is applicable to our own hearts now in that when Jesus Christ is given the proper place in our lives the power of sin is conquered. But this is something only He can do as we are willing to let Him.

Establishing Worship, II Samuel 6

The next great step that took place when David became king was the establishing of Jerusalem as the center of worship for Israel. When the Israelites were in the desert after having left Egypt, God gave them instructions through Moses to build the Tabernacle whose central piece of furniture was the ark. This was an oblong box made of acacia wood, and the top was covered with gold. This in turn was shadowed by two golden cherubims. Inside the ark were the tables of stone of the law, and Aaron's rod that budded. The gold covering was known as the mercy seat and the ark itself signified the presence of God. Concerning this, the Lord said, "There between cherubims on the mercy seat shall my name be."

Today God is not worshipped in any place made with hands. Neither does He identify His special dwelling place on earth with an ark of the covenant. Instead we learn that our bodies are the temple of the Holy Spirit (I Cor. 6:19,20). We are also indwelt by Christ, for Galatians 2:20 says, "I am crucified with Christ: nevertheless I live; yet not I, but Christ liveth in me."

When David first attempted to take the ark into Jerusalem he made a wrong start. There is a wrong way and a right way to do God's will. Some might wonder what difference it makes how we serve the Lord just so we serve Him with all our hearts and strength. David found out there was a difference.

For some time the ark had been kept in the house of Abinadab, so when the Israelites wanted to move it to its new location they thought a new cart drawn by oxen (just as the Philistines had done in the time of Eli) was the best procedure to follow. The responsibility for driving this cart with the ark on it was given to the two sons of Abinadab. David's motives were good in this respect and, without doubt, he was very happy at this development in the plans for making Jerusalem the center of worship as God had intended.

The ark was brought out of the house and placed on the cart and the oxen started on their journey. But the road was rough and the ark was shaken. Fearing it might fall off, Uzzah, a son of Abinadab, put his hand out to steady the ark but was immediately striken dead under the judgment of God. We read, "And the anger of the Lord was kindled against Uzzah; and God smote him there for his error; and there he died by the ark of God" (II Sam. 6:7).

David was very much displeased at this turn of events and was also afraid of the Lord and said, "How shall the ark of the Lord come to me?" (v. 9). For this reason he did not take the ark at that time into the city of Jerusalem, but put it in the house of Obed-edom, the Gittite, where it remained for several months.

The thing David had overlooked was that God had given

specific directions with regard to the moving of the ark. David had followed the pagan Philistines and had not consulted God's Word with respect to this matter. According to Numbers 4:15 the Levites were to carry the ark. The ark representing as it did the presence of God was to be treated with care because God is a holy God.

This teaches us that what we do for the Lord must not be treated as something commonplace. In order to do it right, we need God's favorable presence with us. Almost all things by the law were cleansed with blood, which reminds us that we need the daily cleansing of the blood of Christ as I John 1:7 tells us. Then we must seek to do God's work in His power whether it is preaching a sermon, teaching a lesson or talking with a soul about Christ.

We must be careful always to keep God's message on the high level that He has given it to us. We must not tone it down to suit man's low desires, nor alter it to suit his perverted ideas. We must not tamper with the holiness of God. When we do, we invite judgment. Ananias and Sapphira thought they could serve God through a lie, but that cannot be done.

The Ark of the Covenant was not to be hauled around on an ox cart, but to be carried by the Levitical priests. Long poles were inserted through rings in the ark. These poles were then raised to the shoulders of the priests. In this manner the ark was to be moved. We dare not trifle with God or the things of God. One day I talked to a man of God in his hotel room and asked him about his devotional life. He pointed to the door that led to the corridor in the hotel and said, "I believe that God would strike me dead if I went through that door any day to do the service of the Lord without first having met Him in personal devotions and having my heart and mind purified and cleansed in His presence."

Isaiah had a vision of God in all His holiness and he trembled. Daniel fainted in the presence of the Lord. John, the writer of the Book of the Revelation, fell as one dead when he came into the presence of the Lord. David, too, learned the need of being sanctified before God and not to trifle with God's holiness.

For three months the ark was left in the home of Obed-edom. During that time David must have searched the Word to find out where he had been wrong in moving the ark to begin with. This we learn from I Chronicles 15: "Then David said, None ought to carry the ark of God but the Levites: for them hath the Lord chosen to carry the ark of God, and to minister unto him for ever" (v. 2). David realized that because it had not been taken care of in this way the Lord "made a breach upon us, for that we sought him not after the due order" (v. 13). So the Levites, we are told, sanctified themselves to bring up the ark and they bore it on their shoulders "with the staves thereon, as Moses commanded according to the word of the Lord" (vv. 14,15).

We of this day through faith in Christ are made a kingdom of priests unto God. But we must learn we cannot take lightly the holiness of our God. When we ask His help and ask Him to be with us to sustain us in our service, remember we must have a clean heart and a clean life, one that is washed in the blood of Christ. It is not for us to tone down the Word of God to please sinful man, but through the Author of the gospel to bring men up to God's standards.

When God Said "No," II Samuel 7

This portion opens with these words: "And it came to pass, when the king sat in his house, and the Lord had given him rest round about from all his enemies; That the king said unto Nathan the prophet, See now, I dwell in an house of cedar, but the ark of God dwelleth within curtains" (vv. 1,2).

By this time David had been king some 15 years. With the help of the Lord he had subdued all of Israel's enemies. There was temporary rest in his kingdom. Hiram the King of Tyre had sent cedar wood and all manner of building materials in order that David could build a house for himself in Jerusalem. As David pondered conditions in his kingdom and in his capital city, he called to him Nathan the prophet and said something like this: "I now live in a lovely house, a house of cedars, but God whose presence is marked by the Ark of the Covenant has only a tent. I do not feel right about this. I fear I am giving God second place and myself first place."

To give God second place is a common practice with many of us, but not all have David's conscience on the matter. We give God money if there is any left over. We forget that the cattle on a thousand hills belong to God and all the gold and silver is His. We do not give to Him until we first give ourselves and recognize that all we have belongs to Him. We may even give a tithe of what we receive and still not meet the real standard God has set for us. He allows us to keep a certain amount for our living and to conduct our business but He wants His business to go forward also, and for that He asks our gifts. They must be given to Him first, then we can have our share.

Our time, too, belongs to Him. So often what we give is just what we have left over. Many say, "I just don't have time to do this." Perhaps the greatest thief of time is television. The average American family spends over five hours daily watching television. One person may not spend that much time, but added together the family spends that amount watching. Since it has come into use, the church of Jesus Christ has suffered greatly. There is greater lethargy among God's people and more backsliding than at any time in the memory of some of us. The real problem lies in our having put ourselves first and God second.

Nathan commended David for his desire and then went to his own house. That night God spoke to the prophet, and as an obedient servant Nathan brought the word to David. The message was: "No." God was not going to allow him to build a house of worship for Him. The Lord, however, was pleased with the intentions and the attitude of David's heart in this matter. Years later, after David's death, Solomon built a magnificent temple and in his dedication message said, "It was in the heart of David, my father to build an house for the name of the Lord God of Israel. And the Lord said unto David my father, Whereas it was in thine heart to build an house unto my name, thou didst well that it was in thine heart" (I Kings 8:17,18). David was a man after the heart of God and had set his heart on making God preeminent. Nevertheless, God said to David, "Thou shalt not build the house; but thy son that shall come forth out of thy loins, he shall build the house unto my name. And the Lord hath performed his word that he spake, and I am risen up in the room of David my father, and sit on the throne of Israel, as the Lord promised, and have built an house for the name of the Lord God of Israel" (I Kings 8:18-20).

Though God said "no" to the building of a house, He was so pleased with David's attitude that he made a covenant with David by which He promised to establish the house of David forever. The heart of this covenant is in these words: "And when thy days be fulfilled, and thou shalt sleep with thy fathers, I will set up thy seed after thee, which shall proceed out of thy bowels, and I will establish his kingdom. He shall build an house for my name, and I will stablish the throne of his kingdom for ever" (II Sam. 7:12,13).

In this whole incident we find that David is the same unspoiled humble man that he was in his youth. We remember from the 18th chapter of I Samuel that when Saul offered David his daughter Merab in marriage, David said, "Who am I? and what is my life, or my father's family in Israel, that I should be son in law to the king?" Now the years have gone by and God has established David on the throne and has promised that he will not lack a ruler in his house forever. This ruler is of course the Lord Jesus Christ who shall as King establish the throne of David. When that promise was given, David reacted to it as he did to Saul's. David said, "Who am I, O Lord God? and what is my house, that thou hast brought me hitherto?" By faith he accepted the covenant and humbly accepted also God's "no" to the building of a temple of worship.

Out of this experience of David came a very personal experience of my own. One evening when meditating for my own spiritual help on this passage from II Samuel, I was thinking of it with regard to God's dealing in my own life. When I asked the girl who is now my wife to marry me, I said to her something like this: "Will you go with me to the ends of the earth, publishing the gospel of Jesus Christ?" Her answer was, "I will go with you to the ends of the earth, where-ever God leads and that for the rest of my life."

Our hope and purpose was to work for the Lord on the foreign field. We had prepared for that in our schooling and had made application to several missionary societies.

For a time the Lord led us into the pastorate which seemed to us to be a detour, and then we received word that a mission board had accepted us and was willing to send us out. We went before the Lord searching our hearts to be sure that we were in His will. To our surprise the Lord said "No." This was a little difficult for us to understand, and as the years went by, God opened up this radio ministry of Back to the Bible. This, too, we thought of as being a detour on the road to the foreign field.

We had been in this work seven or eight years when a large missionary society suggested we go to Africa and manage a missionary radio station. My own heart jumped with gladness as I thought I understood now why God had given us this "detour" in gospel radio. God was preparing us through this home ministry for a ministry overseas. We went before the Lord again on the matter, but again God said, "No." Once again this was difficult to understand and hard to take.

We could say, of course, that we were serving the Lord in missionary work through the Broadcast, which was quite true. But as I sat meditating on this portion of II Samuel, the Lord's message to David had a personal message to me. It seemed the Lord was saying to me that He would send my son to the mission field.

This God has done. My son and his wife and family are

in the Philippines. And for good measure, the Lord has one of our daughters and her husband and family in Brazil. This is not to overlook the fact that another daughter is the wife of a pastor here in the United States. We bless God for this and are satisfied to be in His will.

Can you take a "No" from God? He knows what is best for all of us? Remember His promise to David was, "I will be with thee for ever." This promise is ours also for He has said He will never leave us nor forsake us.

CHAPTER THIRTEEN

DAVID'S DARKEST HOUR

II Samuel 11

We have seen before that God does not gloss over the sins of His children. David, though a man after God's own heart, was not sinlessly perfect. We come now to the darkest hour in this great man's life. It seems that the higher the peak of victory, the deeper the fall a believer can sustain. Though David was one of God's choicest men, he gave way to selfish desires that have left a blot on his name time has not erased. I, personally, am frightened at what David did, frightened because none of us are immune to the attacks of sin.

David was no longer a young man. He was fifty years of age and had been king for some 20 years. He had passed through deep trials and testings; but it is possible that the good years as king of Israel had caused him to forget some of the lessons he had learned. He fell—how deep he fell!

We would like to bypass this dark moment, but we dare not. Let us approach it, however, with true humility, in fear and trembling, remembering that we, too, are but dust. The words of Jeremiah in Lamentations need to be indelibly imprinted on our hearts: "This I recall to my mind, therefore have I hope. It is of the Lord's mercies that we are not consumed, because his compassions fail not. They are new every morning: great is thy faithfulness" (Lam. 3:21-23).

Before investigating this period in David's life, we need

to be reminded of God's instructions to Christians with regard to sin and restoration: "If a man be overtaken in a fault, ye which are spiritual, restore such an one in the spirit of meekness; considering thyself, lest thou also be tempted" (Gal. 6:1). Then let us not overlook I Corinthians 10, beginning with verse 11: "Now all these things happened unto them for ensamples: and they are written for our admonition, upon whom the ends of the world are come. Wherefore let him that thinketh he standeth take heed lest he fall."

The divine record of David's great fall begins with these words: "And it came to pass, after the year was expired, at the time when kings go forth to battle, that David sent Joab, and his servants with him, and all Israel; and they destroyed the children of Ammon and besieged Rabbah. But David tarried still at Jerusalem. And it came to pass in an eveningtide, that David arose from off his bed, and walked upon the roof of the king's house: and from the roof he saw a woman washing herself; and the woman was very beautiful to look upon. And David sent and enquired after the woman. And one said, Is not that Bath-sheba, the daughter of Eliam, the wife of Uriah, the Hittite? And David sent messengers, and took her; and she came in unto him, and he lay with her; for she was purified from her uncleanness: and she returned unto her house. And the woman conceived, and sent and told David, and said, I am with child" (II Sam. 11:1-5).

This marks the beginning of the darkest hour in the life of one of God's greatest men. Are we, as we study this, prepared to face sin—not just someone else's sin, but our own? Are we to be appalled at how another man fell under Satan's attack and not be alerted to the danger to our own lives? Peter was writing to us when he said, "Be sober, be vigilant; because your adversary the devil, as a roaring lion, walketh about, seeking whom he may devour: Whom resist stedfast in the faith, knowing that the same afflictions are accomplished in your brethren that are in the world" (I Pet. 5:8,9).

We are warned by the Lord Jesus to "Watch and pray, that ye enter not into temptation" (Matt. 26:41). Like the disciples the spirit may be willing but the flesh is weak. In writing to the Colossians Paul stated: "Continue in prayer, and watch in the same with thanksgiving" (4:2). The writer to the Proverbs warns: "Keep thy heart with all diligence; for out of it are the issues of life" (4:23). Let us not say, "This cannot happen to me. I am able to stand. Nothing will take me away from fellowship with the Lord."

The Lord Jesus gave us the admonition to watch and pray. Many hundreds of times I have prayed and committed myself to the Lord that He might keep my heart and mind centered in the right things. It is not enough to pray. We must also watch—this was where David fell. Perhaps we think the things in our lives that are not what they should be are small compared to the sins of Communism or of the very evil things done in our own country at times. The fact is, our own delinquency is something we must be on guard against.

This sin of David's was recorded for our learning. The Bible does not hesitate to reveal and denounce sin. God's Word conceals nothing. When necessary, it pulls aside the curtain and discloses the human heart. We are stunned as we think of a man like David, wondering how he could have fallen so low. We may even question his salvation. Will God be able to consider him the man after His own heart following this terrible incident? But can we point the finger at David and excuse ourselves?

Are we able to face sin in our own lives, not just David's sin? Our Lord made a very important clarification with regard to the law when He said, "Ye have heard that it was said by them of old time, Thou shalt not commit adultery: But I say unto you, That whosoever looketh on a woman to lust after her hath committed adultery with her already in his heart" (Matt. 5:27,28). Are we ready to face up to this? Do we believe such a passage as I John 3:15 which says, "Whosoever hateth his brother is a murderer: and ye know that no murderer hath eternal life abiding in him"?

David's fall is a confirmation of the solemn fact of man's natural heart condition. Back before the flood, God tells us that He "saw that the wickedness of man was great in the earth, and that every imagination of the thoughts of his heart was only evil continually" (Gen. 6:5). Jeremiah the prophet in his day cried: "The heart is deceitful about all things, and desperately wicked: who can know it?" (Jer. 17:9). Another translation says the heart "is incurable." Paul said, "For I know that in my flesh, dwelleth no good thing" (Rom. 7:18). The human, natural heart is no better now than it was then. Man is still the depraved creature that he became as the result of Adam's sin.

In the case of David we see a man of the household of faith surprised and seduced and led captive by the Devil in an unguarded moment. The flesh in the believer is no different and no better than the flesh in the unbeliever. The sweet singer of Israel still had the old fallen nature in him and so failed at a crucial moment in his life. He did not follow out in his life what could have turned a test into victory. Paul says in Romans 8:13: "If ye live after the flesh, ye shall die: but if ye through the Spirit do mortify the deeds of the body, ye shall live."

Satan is a specialist in glamorizing sin, and David fell into the trap. No wonder David said in Psalm 39:5: "Behold, thou hast made my days as an handbreadth; and mine age is as nothing before thee: verily every man at his best state is altogether vanity."

Imagine with me, if you will, having this conversation with David. "David, you are a man after the heart of God. You have written many beautiful Psalms. You have had many stirring and exceptional experiences. You have walked close with God. You have had your fears and yet you have found God merciful. He has lifted you back to your feet again and again. How then, David, could you fall so low?"

Let David tell us his own story and he will show us the things that led up to this sin. David the great conqueror of Goliath was conquered by his own lusts. The first indication is given in II Samuel 11:1: "And it came to pass, after the year was expired, at the time when kings go forth to battle, that David sent Joab, and his servants with him, and all Israel; and they destroyed the children of Ammon, and besieged Rabbah. But David tarried still at Jerusalem."

David's first answer would be of this nature. "Had I been out fighting the battles of the Lord, I would not have fallen under this temptation. But I was not out there fighting; instead, I was failing God when I should have been directing my troops."

It was the spring of the year when kings begin their military campaigns, or if they are already at war, they renew them. David was a warrior king and ordinarily led his men. It was under his God-directed leadership that Israel became strong. God empowered him and constantly blessed him. David had able generals and delegated part of his military responsibilities to them; but ordinarily, if it was necessary for his armies to be in the field, he was there with them. At this particular time he sent Joab to subdue the Ammonites, "but David tarried still at Jerusalem." In other words, David failed to follow the path of duty. This was one of the steps that led to his terrible fall.

This has a direct message for us. Look at Ephesians 6 beginning with verse 10: "Finally, my brethren, be strong in the Lord, and in the power of his might. Put on the whole armour of God, that ye may be able to stand against the wiles of the devil." Read carefully the next verse in particular: "For we wrestle not [he is speaking about warfare] flesh and blood [it is not man against man], but against principalities, against powers, against the rulers of the darkness of this world, against spiritual wickedness in high places."

We can see from this that the Christian has a battle to fight. But there are too many of us who are not taking part in any battles for the Lord. We may be fighting, but we are fighting our own battles, or we may be fighting the Lord's battles in the wrong way. We fight people, we attack personalities, rather than recognizing that this is a spiritual warfare that goes far deeper than that. Then there are others who say, "We don't have any time to fight such battles."

What do we use our time for? Entertainment? Relaxation? There is a time for rest and recreation, but even in the midst of that we must be fighting the Lord's battles.

David was relaxing when he should have been on the alert. He preferred the luxury of the palace to the hardships of the battlefield. Many of us prefer the luxury of material security and seek that as the first thing to be gained in life instead of putting the will of God first.

David had taken off his armor; consequently, he was without protection. We who fight spiritual enemies dare not lay aside our armor at any time. Our battles are against the darkness of this world, against spiritual wickedness in high places. We cannot withstand the enemy unless we do it in the strength of the Lord.

If we are to stand in the evil day, we need divine help. That time David remained behind in Jerusalem was his evil day, and the Devil caught him off guard. David had on neither his armor for defense nor his weapons of offense. We, too, need offensive armor, the sword of the Spirit and the shoes of the preparation of the gospel of peace, and all prayer.

The Lord tells us to watch and pray, but David rested. He did not watch and he did not pray. We cannot let down our spiritual guard as long as we are in this world. There is no place of rest from this warfare until we stand in the presence of the Lord. And remember, the Lord says watch and pray. This is not only to pray, for prayer without watching would be futile.

In Psalm 91 we learn: "He that dwelleth in the secret place of the most High shall abide under the shadow of the Almighty." Does this infer idleness? No! The whole Psalm speaks of a battle, and the Lord is His people's armor. The Psalmist goes on to say, "I will say of the Lord, He is my refuge and my fortress [these speak of protection]: my God [that suggests offensive warfare]; in him will I trust."

The Psalmist tells us that when the believer is in the front lines that "He [God] shall cover thee with his feathers, and under his wings shalt thou trust: his truth shall be thy shield and buckler." This is divine protection indeed! No wonder then the Psalmist can continue with these encouraging words: "Thou shalt not be afraid for the terror by night; nor for the arrow that flieth by day; Nor for the pestilence that walketh in darkness; nor for the destruction that wasteth at noonday. A thousand shall fall at thy side, and ten thousand at thy right hand; but it shall not come nigh thee" (Ps. 91:5-7).

To the believer who places himself under the protection of God and uses God's offensive weapons in the power of God, these things are true: "Because he hath set his love upon me, therefore will I deliver him: I will set him on high, because he hath known my name." We set our love on God by giving ourselves to Him completely and unreservedly for the spiritual warfare.

Paul spoke of this in Colossians 3 when he said, "If ye then be risen with Christ, seek those things which are above, where Christ sitteth on the right hand of God. Set your affection on things above, not on things upon the earth."

As we study this whole passage and meditate on it, we will find ourselves driven to the bosom of God. Then we will be able to say as Paul said to Timothy: "For I know whom I have believed, and am persuaded that he is able to keep that which I have committed unto him against that day" (II Tim. 1:12). This is more than just a mere act of committal. There must, of course, be an initial committal, but that should continue daily, in fact in moment by moment committal as an attitude: "If any man will come after me, let him deny himself, and take up his cross daily, and follow me."

Paul presented this same truth in writing to Timothy: "But thou, O man of God, flee these things. Follow after righteousness, and godliness, faith, patience, love, meekness." We are to flee one thing and follow after another, to fight the good fight of faith and lay hold on eternal life. We are to flee youthful lusts and to follow righteousness instead (II Tim. 2:22).

This calls for watchfulness and alertness. Let us check

carefully the direction of our desires. Let us probe our motives. We must watch the tendencies of things which in themselves may be lawful but they may not be necessary or advisable; and, if indulged in, could lead us away from God. Unless we are watchful, what seem to be perfectly normal and harmless associations and associates, could lead us astray.

The writer to the Proverbs goes to the very heart of this problem in a few words: "Keep thy heart with all diligence; for out of it are the issues of life" (Prov. 4:23).

I've Anchored in Jesus

Upon life's boundless ocean where mighty billows roll,
I've fixed my hope in Jesus, blest anchor of my soul;
When trials fierce assail me and storms are gath'ring o'er,
I'll rest upon His mercy and trust Him more.

He keeps my soul from evil and gives me blessed peace,
His voice has stilled the waters and bid their tumult cease.
My Pilot and Deliv'rer, to Him I all confide,
For always when I need Him, He's at my side.

He is my Friend and Saviour, in Him my anchor's cast,
He drives away my sorrow and shields me from the blast;
By faith I'm looking upward beyond life's troubled sea,
There I behold a haven prepared for me.

I've anchored in Jesus, the storms of life I'll brave,
I've anchored in Jesus, I'll fear no wind or wave,
I've anchored in Jesus for He hath pow'r to save,
I've anchored to the Rock of Ages.

Slothfulness in Business

As a second thing that led to his downfall, David would point to slothfulness in attending to his affairs. The second verse of the chapter we are studying says, "And it came to pass in an eveningtide, that David arose from off his bed, and walked upon the roof of the king's house: and from the roof he saw a woman washing herself [bathing herself]; and the woman was very beautiful to look upon." The Bible hides nothing from us, but in exposing sin it does not make sin attractive or glamorous.

There are times when any of us need physical refreshing. We may need to rest for a few minutes, but David was going far beyond this, and was not attending to his business at all. He was not watchful. Being in the midst of spiritual warfare allows us no time for slothfulness. We need to constantly take to ourselves the whole armor of God so that we may be able to withstand in the evil day and having done all to stand.

A good illustration of a man who attended to business was Nehemiah when he was directing the rebuilding of the walls of Jerusalem. Some of Israel's foes came to him and said, "Come let us meet together in some one of the villages in the plains of Ono, but they thought to do him mischief. And I sent messengers unto them, I am doing a great work, so I cannot come down: why should the work cease, whilst I leave it, and come down to you?" Nehemiah was a man who knew what was right, and how to guard himself against the intrigues of men such as Sanballat and Geshem.

We have often heard the saying, "The idle mind is the Devil's workshop." Idleness was one of the things that led to the sins and the final downfall of Sodom and Gomorrah. Ezekiel the prophet wrote: "Behold, this was the iniquity of thy sister Sodom, pride, fulness of bread, and abundance of idleness was in her and in her daughters, neither did she strengthen the hand of the poor and needy" (Ezek. 16:49). Idleness! Slothfulness! A good soldier of Jesus Christ cannot afford to be idle in spiritual things.

Unguarded Eyes

In the third place, if David were to tell us what led to his downfall, he would say, "I will have to blame my eyes. I accidently beheld a woman taking a bath on a house roof, and instead of turning my eyes away from her, I watched her and saw that she was beautiful."

There is danger in some of the things we see especially if we continue to look at them. Some things perhaps we cannot avoid seeing once, but we need not look at them twice. John warns us: "For all that is in the world, the lust of the flesh, and the lust of the eyes, and the pride of life, is not of the Father" (I John 2:16). The lusts of the flesh is the old nature that is ever in man, even the believer, as long as he is in his physical body. Only through the power of the Holy Spirit can that nature be conquered; so we need to be careful of what we see. The evil nature in us can use such things to trip us up.

James tells us, "And every man is tempted when he is drawn away of his own lust, and enticed. Then when lust hath conceived, it bringeth forth sin; and sin, when it is finished, bringeth forth death" (James 1:14,15).

This is illustrated for us in the seventh chapter of Joshua where we learn that when Achan was confronted with his sin and called on to confess it he said, "Indeed I have sinned against the Lord God of Israel, and thus and thus have I done: When I saw among the spoils"—his downfall started with what he saw. First he saw a good Babylonish garment, and then silver, then what his eyes beheld, he wanted, he coveted; and then he took them; finally he hid them. One trouble with sin is that it will not stay hidden. "Be sure your sin will find you out." The very thing we may try to cover up will finally lead to our exposure.

The Psalmist cries in Psalm 119:37: "Turn away mine eyes from beholding vanity." He knew by experience what this could do to a life. We might well follow Job's example when he said, "I made a covenant with mine eyes, why then should I look upon a maid?" We need to be careful what we look at. Let us covenant with God to control our eyes so that we do not desire the wrong things. The Lord Jesus spoke about the danger of lustful eyes when He said, "Ye have heard that it was said by them of old time, thou shalt not commit adultery: But I say unto you, That whosoever looketh [the eyes again] on a woman to lust after her hath committed adultery with her already in his heart. And if thy right eye offend thee, pluck it out, and cast it from thee: for it is profitable for thee that one of thy members should perish, and not that thy whole body should be cast into hell" (Matt. 5:27-29). It is very necessary that we learn to discipline our bodies, in this case the eye, as the Bible instructs us.

In one of His discourses, the Lord referred again to the eye in these words: "The light of the body is the eye: therefore when thine eye is single, thy whole body also is full of light; but when thine eye is evil, thy body also is full of darkness. Take heed therefore that the light which is in thee be not darkness" (Luke 11:34). The Lord said here that the eye is that which allows light into the mind, but if we look on the wrong things, we will use our eyes to bring darkness to our souls. This is exactly what happened in the life of David.

The eye gate, as we sometimes call it, is neither good nor bad in itself, it depends on how it is used by us. We are told that we learn much more through the eye gate than through the ear gate; this should alert us to be careful of what we look at. We are living in an age that has gone mad after sex. Part of this trend is promoted through pictures in magazines, on magazine covers, on book covers, and in many other ways. We need to turn our eyes away from beholding vanity. This was what the Psalmist learned. It is the admonition we need also.

Sin Premeditated

Up to this point, David had been lazy and slothful in his work. Then he let his desires drive him into deliberate, premeditated sin. He asked his servants who the woman was and one said, "Is this not Bath-sheba, the daughter of Eliam, the wife of Uriah the Hittite?" Then it was that David "sent messengers, and took her; and she came in unto him, and he lay with her; for she was purified from her uncleanness: and she returned unto her house." To accidently see this woman was one thing, but to desire after her was something else. He could have asked God to take over in his life and deliver him from this evil, but he did not ask. God also saw to it that David was reminded Bath-sheba was another man's wife and this in itself should have warned the king to the wrong direction he was taking. Instead, he saw; he desired; he inquired; and then he sinned, and sin brought forth death. Sin never brings forth life, only death. And one sin seldom remains alone. It accumulates other sins. The course of sin in the church age can be viewed in Revelation chapters 2 and 3 where we learn that in the first phase of its existence the church left its first love. When we come to the last part we find God saying that He would spew it out of His mouth.

David's sin of adultery was not the end of his fall. It led him to commit murder also. David sank into spiritual deadness with no apparent thought of repentance until God shook him to the very depths of his soul, and he returned to his senses and sought God's forgiveness.

It does not seem that David's sin was necessarily a sin of a moment. The affair with Bath-sheba was the climax of 20 years of looseness with regard to the warnings of God concerning kings. In Deuteronomy 17:16,17 the Lord warned Israel's leaders that they should not multiply horses nor lay up to themselves silver and gold nor multiply to themselves wives. David was careful about two of these things. He did not go in for raising horses and what gold and silver he laid up was for the purpose of building a house for God. But in the third realm David failed. He had many wives. Michal, Saul's daughter was his first wife. Then he married Abigail, the widow of Nabal, then Ahinoam of Jezreel. While living at Hebron, he took to himself four more wives. Then, when he moved his home to Jerusalem, he added more wives and concubines.

These rules for the kings of Israel were given so that they might discipline themselves and be saved from the very thing that caused David's downfall. His sin with Bath-sheba was more than the passion of a moment, because for 20 years he had been sowing the seeds of fleshly indulgence, and they now ended in this terrible iniquity.

Sin Pays Wages

Perhaps in the days and weeks that followed David thought his sin with Bath-sheba would be nothing more than a passing incident and soon be forgotten. But whatever he thought about it, he was rudely shaken by a message which she sent to him. She told him, "I am with child." In a situation like this we cannot help but think of such passages as Numbers 32:23: "Be sure your sin will find you out," or Hebrews 11:25: "The pleasures of sin are but for a season." This was a short season indeed for the king of Israel. He began to learn the truth of the Proverb that sin like intoxicating wine "biteth like a serpent, and stingeth like an adder" (Prov. 23:32).

David's sin was out and the time of reckoning was upon him. The law was very specific with regard to the sin of adultery. Moses wrote in Leviticus 20:10: "And the man that committeth adultery with another man's wife, even he that committeth adultery with his neighbour's wife, the adulterer and adulteress shall surely be put to death." According to the law, David, though king of Israel, should by rights have been stoned to death. The sin was primarily his; no accusation is made against Bath-sheba. David's power was practically absolute, and what he demanded he received. Whether Bath-sheba was willing or unwilling, she had no other alternative but to obey or suffer the consequences of the king's anger.

David found himself in a bad fix. Uriah was away at war fighting some of David's battles, so David's sin could not be kept under cover. If Uriah found out his wife's condition, and if he brought it to the attention of the elders of Israel, David might lose his kingdom. He might also have lost his life.

David was aware of the consequences and resorted to carnal methods to cover his sin. The Bible is very plain on this point, however. "He that covereth his sins shall not prosper: but whoso confesseth and forsaketh them shall have mercy" (Prov. 28:13). As David looked at the matter, he considered that at stake were his reputation, his kingdom and his name, so he resorted to a scheme which led him deeper into sin.

First of all, David sent word to Joab, "Send me Uriah the Hittite. And Joab sent Uriah to David." David's first scheme was to bring Uriah home on a military furlough hoping that Uriah would be considered the father of Bathsheba's child.

This man Uriah, however, was an unusual man, being counted among the first 36 of David's great men. He was a warrior devoted to his king and to his country. When Uriah came to him, David asked how Joab did and how the war prospered just as though he had brought Uriah home to report on the course of the war. Then David dismissed him saying, "Go down to your house, and wash thy feet. And Uriah departed out of the king's house." David then sent food to his home, but instead of going home, Uriah slept at the door of the king's house with David's servants.

Uriah was much more righteous than David in this. He would permit himself of no relaxation until the war was over.

When it was told David that Uriah had not gone to his own house, David asked him, "Camest thou not from thy journey? why then didst thou not go down unto thine house?" It was as if David were asking him if he were sociable or if things were not all right between him and his wife. David intimated that since Uriah was one of his generals, one of his big men, he was entitled to this time of leisure.

Uriah's answer must have startled David: "The ark, and Israel, and Judah, abide in tents; and my lord Joab, and the servants of my Lord, are encamped in the open fields; shall I then go into mine house, to eat and to drink, and to lie with my wife? As thou livest, and as thy soul liveth, I will not do this thing." Could we find a better example of consecration? Here was a man who would not let the normal and permissable things of life come between him and his responsibilities to the living God.

This put David in a quandary. His original scheme had failed, and he needed time to think of another. So he said to Uriah, "Tarry here to day also, and to morrow I will let thee depart. So Uriah abode in Jerusalem that day, and the morrow" (v. 12). David tried another plan. This was another example of one sin leading to another. He called Uriah before him and had him eat and drink until he became drunk. An intoxicated man will do things that he would not do when sober. He will commit sins that he would avoid at other times. Strong drink and sexual excesses often go together. David hoped through this that Uriah would go to his own home. This, then, was David's plan, and it proved that when David was under the control of his fallen nature he was no better than the worst of sinners. And neither are we when ruled by our fallen natures, for our Adamic natures are unchangeably evil.

David next resorted to extreme measures. To the sin of adultery he added the sin of murder. He wrote a letter to Joab and sent it by the hand of Uriah with instructions that Uriah must meet death in battle. Here was this man, honest, upright, fully dedicated to his nation and to his king, who was given a letter with his own death warrant in it to be handed to Joab the leader of Israel's army. David wrote saying, "Set ye Uriah in the forefront of the hottest battle, and retire ye from him, that he may be smitten, and die" (v. 15). In this way if David could not cover up his sin with a stratagem, then he would seal Uriah's lips so that he could not deny he was the father of Bath-sheba's child.

We are not told what Joab's personal reactions were, but he obeyed his king. Uriah died in battle as David had ordered. It is possible that being the kind of man he was, Joab found some evil humor in the situation. His own hands were not clean, for he had killed Abner the general of the Israelite army in a manner that was only thinly disguised murder. Perhaps he thought now that he had something on David so that David could never point the finger of accusation at him and say, "You killed Abner." David had put himself in Joab's power by the murder of Uriah.

When Bath-sheba heard that her husband was dead, she mourned for him. At the end of her time of mourning David sent for her, and she became his wife.

Perhaps David now felt that everything would be covered

up and that his and Bath-sheba's child would be born without any stain being attached to David's name. In all this, David reckoned without the Lord, for we read in II Samuel 11: "But the thing that David had done displeased the Lord."

Let me say this, though I say it with fear and trembling. David's actions in trying to cover up his own personal guilt of adultery by murder put him in the same class as Pilate who crucified Jesus Christ to satisfy the people. Pilate thought that by washing his hands he could cleanse himself of any guilt in connection with the judicial murder of the Lord Jesus Christ. And apparently David thought that in bringing Bath-sheba into his harem he was covering up his sin of adultery and of the judicial murder of Uriah. There is a marked difference in the future of these men following their crimes. Pilate, we are told in secular history, committed suicide. David, we learn from the sacred record, was restored to fellowship with the Lord though he never fully got beyond the consequences of the train of evil circumstances he had started. They plagued him and his family and his kingdom to the end of his life.

We must never forget that the evil nature in the believer or the flesh nature as it is sometimes called, the nature inherited from Adam, is no different in us than in the unbeliever. Until we see this, we will never understand the sovereign grace of God and God's sovereignty in the methods he uses in handling our lives.

Some of us think that when a person like David falls into such terrible sin, the reason must be that he was not a true believer as yet. But this does not face up to the teaching of Scripture nor does it help us when we get into difficulties with sins in our lives. Jesus Christ did not come to save the old flesh nature, or to make it any better, or to train it to behave itself, or even to give it favorable recognition. The old man is crucified with Christ. We learn through the Scriptures and then in our experience to hold the attitude of being dead to sin. This we do by the grace of God, recognizing that in our flesh nature there is no good thing.

Our Lord Jesus Christ was different from the rest of us in this that He did not inherit a sinful nature from Adam. He was "that holy thing" which was born of the virgin. There was no sin in Him at any time. He was flawless. Though He was tested in all points like as we are, yet He himself was without sin.

This flesh nature was in David just as it is in everyone else. This flesh nature is in everyone of us who have trusted in Christ as personal Saviour. God did not change the old nature in us when He saved us from sin, but He gave us the means whereby we could constantly consider ourselves dead to the flesh. The flesh is crucified with Christ. The lust of the eye sought satisfaction in David and the flesh nature took over and he sinned. After he sinned the pride of life showed itself. He wanted to hold on to his reputation and to his position, and this led him to committing the awful murder of Uriah. This is the kind of thing John spoke of in his first letter when he spoke of the lust of the flesh and the lust of the eye and the pride of life.

David did not begin his downward steps with murderous designs in his heart. It was simply the lust of the flesh, the satisfying of his evil nature that he had in mind. But he had started on a path that leads to death, as James says, "Every man is tempted, when he is drawn away of his own lust, and enticed. Then when lust hath conceived, it bringeth forth sin: and sin, when it is finished, bringeth forth death."

David learned the truth of the proverb that he who covers his sin shall not prosper "but whoso confesseth and forsaketh them shall have mercy" (Prov. 28:13). David found himself not prospering. His guilty conscience estranged him from Almighty God. Later, when David wrote Psalm 32 and told of his condition at this time, he said, "When I kept silent, my bones waxed old through my roaring all the day long. For day and night thy hand was heavy upon me: my moisture is turned into the drought of summer" (vv. 3,4). This was David's description of his condition when he was out of fellowship with the Lord and committed one sin after another. He found God's hand was heavy upon him, but God did not turn him loose. Why? Because David was still a child of God. God chastens His child when necessary and disciplines him when the situation calls for it, but He does not disown him.

The 12th chapter of Hebrews makes this very clear: "My son, despise not thou the chastening of the Lord, nor faint when thou art rebuked of him: For whom the Lord loveth he chasteneth, and scourgeth every son whom he receiveth" (vv. 5,6). David's conscience was heavy during this time because God was dealing with him. God at no time glosses over our sins or counts them as small.

Perhaps we think that this will never happen to us, but do not be so sure. God will keep us from evil such as this if we will commit ourselves to Him; but we must determine moment by moment to walk in fellowship with Him. Let us remember that the old Devil is still going around like a roaring lion seeking to devour whomever he can. He is looking for a believer who is off guard. David was off guard for a little and Satan found the weakness in his life and led him on from sin to sin.

Remember Paul's admonition in I Corinthians 10. This is an inspired admonition. The Holy Spirit himself tells us that these Old Testament incidents were written as examples for our admonition "upon whom the ends of the world are come. Wherefore let him that thinketh he standeth take heed lest he fall. Wherefore, my dearly beloved, flee from idolatry. I speak as to wise men; judge ye what I say."

Let me remind you again of the high standard our Saviour held toward the law. It is not only the person who commits physical adultery who is an adulterer. If a man looks on a woman to lust after her he has already committed adultery in his heart. It is not always what we do but also how we think, and how we desire. Let us not be so positive that these things could not happen to us.

CHAPTER FOURTEEN

GOD'S DISPLEASURE WITH DAVID'S SIN

II Samuel 12

"The thing that David had done displeased the Lord" are the closing words of II Samuel 11. David had committed other wrongs in his life. He had lied, had pouted, had played the fool, had been quick tempered; but after his death God said of David: "Because David did that which was right in the eyes of the Lord, and turned not aside from any thing that he commanded him all the days of his life, save only in the matter of Uriah, the Hittite" (I Kings 15:5). This sin is singled out as the one great element of displeasure that God had in David's life.

There are several reasons why his sin was so grievous to God. In Hebrews 13:4 God's comment on marriage is, "Marriage is honourable in all, and the bed undefiled: but whoremongers and adulterers God will judge." The reason why this is so is given in I Corinthians 6:18: "Flee fornication. Every sin that a man doeth is without the body; but he that committeth fornication sinneth against his own body. What! know ye not that your body is the temple [the holy of holies] of the Holy Ghost which is in you, which ye have of God, and ye are not your own?" The body of every believer is the Lord's for His personal habitation. God's holy of holies is identified with the body so that if the sin of adultery is committed, then that which is holy to God has been made one with a harlot or a whoremonger.

Another reason for David's sin being so grievous was that

it was premeditated and deliberate. In the main, David's thought was usually for the honor of God, but in committing this sin, he gave into the basest form of selfishness.

Finally, it was a sin that gave the enemies of God an excuse to blaspheme. This was true not only of David's day but has been true through succeeding generations. Some men have used it as an excuse for being hardened in their infidelity. Still others have been encouraged by it to hide their wickedness under a religious cloak. All in all, David's sin has brought discredit to the gospel of Jesus Christ.

Nevertheless, during all this time God was waiting for an opportunity to awaken David to the seriousness of his spiritual lapse. Then the opportunity came. God sent Nathan to David (II Sam. 12:1). God calls for holy boldness in His servants, but there is a vast difference between this and the modern-day slandering and murdering of character which sometimes goes on in Christian circles. It took a man bold in the Lord to face King David with his terrible crimes.

That David's heart was not unprepared for Nathan's visit, however, is hinted at in several passages. We have already read in Psalm 32 how David said that when he kept silence his bones waxed old through his roaring all the day long. Day and night God's hand was heavy upon him. Why this was so is given in Psalm 50:21, one of Asaph's Psalms: "These things hast thou done, and I kept silence; thou thoughtest that I was altogether such an one as thyself: but I will reprove thee, and set them in order before thine eyes." God says here that He is not going to sit quietly by and let His child go on in sin indefinitely.

The child of God who goes into sin does not have a pleasant life. "Bread of deceit is sweet to a man; but afterwards his mouth shall be filled with gravel" (Prov. 20:17). This David found out. David's condition was also expressed clearly by Jeremiah at a later date when he said in Lamentations 3:7: "He hath hedged me about, that I cannot get out: he hath made my chain heavy." Jeremiah was speaking here of Israel, but it well expresses David's heart condition. It will be true of us also if we are children of God and have fallen into deep sin. If any person can sin deeply and never have that sin bother him, then I would doubt greatly if such an one is a child of God. God will never allow His children to go on unhindered on a sinful path.

Matthew Henry once said, "Though God may suffer His people to fall into sin, He will not suffer His people to lie still in sin."

Turning to Lamentations again we find these words: "Also when I cry and shout, he shutteth out my prayer." God won't listen to us when we are in sin. "He hath turned aside my ways, and pulled me in pieces: he hath made me desolate" (3:11). In verse 15 of the same chapter we read, "He hath filled me with bitterness, he hath made me drunken with wormwood." The lament continues: "He hath also broken my teeth with gravel stones, he hath covered me with ashes. And thou hast removed my soul far off from peace: I forgat prosperity." Then in verse 21 comes a new note: "This I recall to my mind, therefore have I [still] hope. It is of the Lord's mercies that we are not consumed, because his compassions fail not. They are new every morning: great is thy faithfulness." God is speaking here, of course, of His children and of His manner of disciplining them.

Someone has said that a king may command his subjects but he cannot quiet the voice of an outraged conscience. This is what we have learned from David as he felt God's hand heavy upon him. Then the time came for God to seek David's restoration.

God might have disciplined David by sending an enemy against him, or He could have sent some severe affliction upon him, instead God sent a prophet to him. This was grace. Though he had fallen far, he was still God's child. Some of us are not big enough to believe this; our understanding of the grace of God is not large enough to conceive of such mercy. But let us not forget that Psalm 37 says: "The steps of a good man are ordered by the Lord; and he delighteth in his way. Though he fall, he shall not be utterly cast down: for the Lord upholdeth him with his hand" (vv. 23,24). The righteous man here is not necessarily one who has done righteousness all the time, but one who is righteous in his position before God because he has accepted God's righteousness in Christ.

This is the only explanation we can offer for such a passage as II Timothy 2:13 where the inspired apostle writes: "If we believe not [if we fail him], yet he abideth faithful: he cannot deny himself." He does not mean He is going to pass over sin, but He will not allow us to remain in the sinful condition.

In Psalm 89, beginning with verse 20, we read: "I have found David my servant; with my holy oil have I anointed him: With whom my hand shall be established: mine arm also shall strengthen him." Beginning with verse 30 are these words: "If his children [God is talking about other generations] forsake my law, and walk not in my judgments; If they break my statutes, and keep not my commandments; Then will I visit their transgressions with the rod, and their iniquity with stripes. Nevertheless, my lovingkindness will I not utterly take from him, nor suffer my faithfulness to fail. My covenant will I not break, nor alter the things that is gone out of my lips. Once have I sworn by my holiness that I will not lie unto David. His seed shall endure for ever, and his throne as the sun before me. It shall be established for ever as the moon, and as a faithful witness in heaven. Selah." That last word means "Think about this." This is God's covenant with David and He will not break it.

God has made a covenant with us. When we became His children He said of each of us, "I took you into my hands, and into my arms, and no man is going to take you out of my hands" (Paraphrase of John 10:28,29). Now, this does not mean that He is not going to allow us to suffer for our sins. We have much to learn from David's sin; but one of the things we should remember is that God does not lightly pass over sin in His children. Neither will He allow them to continue long in it.

So in all this God displays first His holiness, showing His

hatred for sin and bringing the guilty one to repent of it and confess it. In the second place, God displays His righteousness by visiting chastisement upon His sinful child, more of which we shall see in later studies. In the third place, we see that God demonstrates His mercy in leading a backslidden child to forsake his sin, and to find pardon at the hands of his Heavenly Father. This is why we read in Psalm 85:10: "Mercy and truth are met together [truth exposes the sin, but mercy forgives it]; righteousness and peace have kissed each other." This is God's approach to the subject.

Coming back again to Nathan and the task God placed upon him, we see that he was called on for faithfulness to God in the face of his king's possible displeasure. This should remind us that we need to pray for God's servants at all times.

In the New Testament we are told that if a man is overtaken in a fault, those who are spiritual are to restore such a person in the spirit of meekness, considering themselves lest they also be tempted. Nathan was careful in his approach, and under the direction of God chose an indirect way to help awaken the conscience of David. It was also done in such a way as to cause David to pass sentence against himself without being fully aware of it.

Nathan "came unto David and said unto him, There were two men in one city; the one rich, and the other poor. The rich man had exceeding many flocks and herds: But the poor man had nothing, save one little ewe lamb, which he had bought and nourished up: and it grew up together with him, and with his children; it did eat of his own meat, and drank of his own cup, and lay in his bosom, and was unto him as a daughter. And there came a traveller unto the rich man, and he spared to take of his own flock and of his own herd, to dress for the wayfaring man that was come unto him; but took the poor man's lamb, and dressed it for the man that was come to him." David's reaction was immediate. His "anger was greatly kindled against the man; and he said to Nathan, As the Lord liveth, the man that hath done this thing shall surely die: And he shall restore the lamb fourfold, because he did this thing, and because he had no pity" (vv. 5,6). David's response is without pity as he condemns the rich man who had stolen the lamb from the poor man. It seems to be very easy for us to condemn another for committing wrongs similar to what we ourselves have done. David, in condemning the offender, condemned himself. David was still out of touch with God so that his judgment of death was greater than the law required. To restore fourfold was in accordance with the law but nothing was said of death.

David's harshness and lack of pity were due to his being out of touch with God. No wonder he failed to discern the judgments of the law. It was right at this point that the Holy Spirit gave boldness to Nathan to say to David, "Thou art the man" (v. 7). Before David could recover from the shock of this charge, Nathan continued: "Thus saith the Lord God of Israel, I anointed thee king over Israel, and I delivered thee out of the hand of Saul; And I gave thee thy master's house, and thy master's wives into thy bosom, and gave thee the house of Israel and of Judah; and if that had been too little, I would moreover have given unto thee such and such things. Wherefore hast thou despised the commandment of the Lord, to do evil in his sight? thou hast killed Uriah the Hittite with the sword, and hast taken his wife to be thy wife, and hast slain him with the sword of the children of Ammon" (vv. 7-9).

Through the prophet the Lord reminded David of His sovereign choice with regard to David, of His protection of David through the years of Saul's bitter enmity, of David's elevation to the throne, and of the abundance of God's provision for him. In spite of God's mercies, David had despised God's commandment. God hid nothing from His servant. David was forced to face his sin, fair and square.

Perhaps it was after meditating on this experience that David said in Psalm 139: "O Lord, thou hast searched me, and known me. Thou knowest my downsitting and mine uprising, thou understandest my thought afar off. Thou compassest my path and my lying down, and art acquainted with all my ways" (vv. 1-3). David realized how thoroughly God had sifted his life and examined every area of it, and acknowledged, "there is not a word in my tongue, but, lo, O Lord, thou knowest it altogether. Thou hast beset me behind and before, and laid thine hand upon me. Such knowledge is too wonderful for me; it is high, I cannot attain unto it. Whither shall I go from thy spirit? or whither shall I flee from thy presence? . . . If I say, Surely the darkness shall cover me; even the night shall be light about me. Yea, the darkness hideth not from thee; but the night shineth as the day; the darkness and the light are both alike to thee" (vv. 4-12). David thought the darkness would conceal his sin with Bathsheba and his murder of Uriah, but darkness conceals nothing from God.

David also discovered that God knew what controlled him and that it was God who had made him to be different from others. Here are David's words: "For thou hast possessed my reins: thou hast covered me in my mother's womb. I will praise thee; for I am fearfully and wonderfully made" (vv. 13,14).

After enumerating these various things, David concluded this portion of the Psalm with the words: "Surely thou wilt slay the wicked, O God: depart from me therefore, ye bloody men. For they speak against thee wickedly, and thine enemies take thy name in vain" (vv. 19,20). David saw the wickedness of other lives and hated the wickedness in his own life. So at the very conclusion of the Psalm he cried out: "Search me, O God, and know my heart: try me, and know my thoughts: And see if there be any wicked way in me, and lead me in the way everlasting" (vv. 23,24). How much we need to take these words to our own hearts and let them speak to us as they did to God's servant of old.

Nathan's message to David not only reminded him of God's tender mercy, love, abundance of gifts and honor, but he also warned David that as he had sowed sin, he would reap a harvest of sorrow. "Now therefore the sword shall never depart from thine house; because thou hast despised me, and hast taken the wife of Uriah the Hittite to be thy wife. Thus saith the Lord, Behold, I will raise up evil against thee out of thine own house, and I will take thy wives before thine eyes, and give them unto thy neighbour, and he shall lie with thy wives in the sight of this sun. For thou didst it secretly: but I will do this thing before all Israel, and before the sun" (vv. 10-12).

The Lord makes it very plain in the New Testament that we as believers cannot escape reaping the kind of harvest we sow. To the Galatians Paul wrote: "Be not deceived; God is not mocked: for whatsoever a man soweth, that shall he also reap" (6:7). We may fall into sin but we cannot hide it. We will not get away with it. The secrets of the night are not hidden from God. This truth is clear from both Testaments.

But someone asks, "What about God's forgiveness? When a man's heart is really broken with conviction and he turns back to God calling sin what God has called sin, must that man still reap what he sowed? Is there no mercy with God?"

The Scriptures have the answer for us. Let us read on and see what happened. "And David said unto Nathan, I have sinned against the Lord" (v. 13). David had sinned against Bath-sheba, and against Uriah, and against Joab in making him an accomplice in Uriah's murder, and David had sinned against his own house; but here he acknowledged: "My sin is against thee."

Nathan answered, "The Lord also hath put away thy sin; thou shalt not die." Does this mean that God is going to overlook David's awful sin? Was David a pet to whom God was showing partiality? No indeed! Any of us can have the same forgiveness and the same cleansing if we return to God as David did when he sinned. John wrote: "If we confess our sins, he is faithful and just to forgive us our sins, and to cleanse us from all unrighteousness" (I John 1:9). David received immediate forgiveness, immediate cleansing, immediate restoration, and fellowship—but there also followed suffering as a consequence of his sin.

This is an area in David's life overlooked by his critics. He was dealt with severely by God for his sins, but he responded in a way that showed he deeply repented of them. In a number of the Psalms known as the "penitential psalms" David lays bare his heart before God. With reference to his sin of adultery with Bath-sheba and his murder of Uriah, Psalm 51 is especially significant. Here we learn how David went to the Lord with his sin and how God dealt with him in the light of his repentance. What follows is but an outline of the truths imbedded in this wonderful portion of God's Word. Even this, however, will help answer the questions raised concerning David's repentance and God's forgiveness. It will also help us meet the great issue of sin in our own lives.

Psalm 51

In the first six verses we see sin thoroughly judged before God. David cried, "Have mercy upon me, O God, according to thy lovingkindness: according unto the multitude of thy tender mercies blot out my transgressions" (v. 1). This is a cry for mercy, the only cry that a sinner can make and the only cry that a sinning saint can make. God's grace comes into view later on when the subject of service is raised.

For God to blot out our transgressions means they are put clear out of the way and that we stand justified before God. In the following verse, two thoughts are projected: "Wash me thoroughly from mine iniquity, and cleanse me from my sin." In asking for thorough washing, David was pleading for complete purity. Cleansing has to do with the motives of our actions. David wanted to have the flesh nature, the old nature, subdued and conquered in his heart and life. In this connection it is good to remember again I John 1:9: "If we confess our sins, he is faithful and just to forgive us our sins, and to cleanse us from all unrighteousness."

In verse 3 we see the need for acknowledging our sin before God. If we try to hide it, we will not prosper. When we acknowledge it, we bring it into the open: "For I acknowledge my transgressions: and my sin is ever before me."

Here David said, "Against thee, thee only, have I sinned." It is true that David had some things to straighten out with others, but the sin question had first to be taken care of with God. Sin is more than wrong we do to other human beings; it is first of all sin against God. David says, in effect in this portion: "This sin is against you. When you, Lord, speak, you can judge me properly because it is in your sight, and against you that I have sinned."

David then acknowledged the source of sin in verse 5. He was not excusing himself when he said, "Behold, I was shapen in iniquity; and in sin did my mother conceive me." The word "sin" here was reference to the "old man" or "old nature" which Adam bequeathed to the race and with which each one of us is born. That nature is the root of sin, and though we are not responsible for it, we are responsible for the sins that we commit when we let that fallen nature direct our lives. In order for sinful acts to cease, we must have inner victory over the source of sin. This is what God deals with and this is what David prayed for.

Verse 6 says, "Behold, thou desirest truth in the inward parts: and in the hidden part thou shalt make me to know wisdom." It is not enough to seek forgiveness as an external matter. God is concerned with the outward appearance of things, but He is also concerned with our innermost condition. Saul wanted forgiveness when Samuel pointed out his sin to him, but Saul merely wanted to be justified in the sight of the people. He saw no need of inward cleansing. This, of course, can only be done through Christ.

Familiar to many of us are the words, "Purge me with hyssop, and I shall be clean: wash me, and I shall be whiter than snow" (v. 7). First comes forgiveness and cleansing by the blood. This is purging. This is basic to salvation. Following this there is a washing by the Word of God itself. In I John 1:9 the cleansing spoken of would have reference to cleansing by the water of the Word.

These two ideas, purging and cleansing, are very clearly illustrated for us in John 13. Jesus took a towel and began to wash the disciples' feet. When he came to Peter, Peter said, "Thou shalt never wash my feet."

The Lord answered: "If I wash thee not, thou hast no part with me." Peter's reply was typical of that apostle. "Lord, not my feet only, but also my hands and my head."

The Lord's answer is very significant. He said, "He that is washed [purged with hyssop, cleansed by the blood] needeth not save to wash his feet, but is clean every whit: and ye are clean, but not all."

What He said was that all of them were born again with the exception of one. A person who is born again does not need to be born again and again. He just needs his "feet washed" which signifies the daily cleansing needed for defilement contracted in the believer's everyday experiences of life.

This truth is referred to in Ephesians 5:25,26: "Christ also loved the church, and gave himself for it; That he might sanctify and cleanse it with the washing of water by the word."

David asked God to create in him a clean heart (v. 10). With regard to the unbeliever, this would be a matter of regeneration but with the Christian it would be renewal and restoration as well. Then he pleaded that he might be filled with the Spirit of God.

In verse 11 is a truth that some have tried to stay away from, possibly because they have not understood its real significance. David said, "Cast me not away from thy presence; and take not thy Holy Spirit from me." We have considered this briefly before, but reference to it again will be valuable. This is Old Testament doctrine and has to do with the fact that when a person had the Spirit of God, and that person was disobedient, the Holy Spirit might leave him as He left Saul. David did not want this to happen to him.

In this church age we learn that the Spirit of God comes into our life to stay. Nevertheless, there are many Christians, some of them Christian workers, who have been put on the shelf and are useless to God because of some kind of sin that they have allowed to control or dominate their lives. Our position before God in Christ is assured; but our condition or experience, if it is to be victorious, must be one of living fellowship with the Lord.

The next verse speaks of the restoration of joy in salvation and of being upheld by God's free spirit. It is then that the grace of God comes into full view as we see David saying, "Then will I teach transgressors thy ways; and sinners shall be converted unto thee." Once the individual has been restored to fellowship, the joy of salvation in his heart, and the Holy Spirit controlling his life, then, by the grace of God, that one can effectively tell others the story of the gospel.

In verse 16 we have these revealing words: "For thou desirest not sacrifice; else would I give it: thou delightest not in burnt-offering. The sacrifices of God are a broken spirit: a broken and a contrite heart, O God, thou wilt not despise." The word "contrite" means a spirit broken down with grief and repentance for sin—a sorry, bruised and broken heart. This was the condition of David's heart after having sinned against the Lord. Whether Psalm 51 was spoken in the presence of Nathan, or afterwards, we do not know, but it fits right at this point in David's life.

In this Psalm we see where David committed himself entirely to the Lord. He confessed his sin and held nothing back, therefore, God immediately forgave him. This was what Nathan meant when he said to David, "The Lord also hath put away thy sin; thou shalt not die" (II Sam. 12:13). Again let us emphasize the fact that there is immediate forgiveness, immediate cleansing, immediate restoration to fellowship, and also the immediate suffering of the consequences of the sins committed.

Cleanse Me

Search me, O God, and know my heart today;
Try me, O Saviour, know my thoughts, I pray:
See if there be some wicked way in me:
Cleanse me from ev'ry sin, and set me free.

CHAPTER FIFTEEN

DAVID CHASTENED OF GOD

David knew, that in reaping the harvest of his sins, he was not paying the price of judgment on those sins. That was paid by Christ himself. Consequently, when a person believes or trusts in Christ for salvation, "there is no more condemnation of sin to them who are in Christ Jesus." The chastening hand of God is designed to purify the life but no amount of chastening could ever remove the guilt of sin. Chastening is for those who are already God's children through faith in Christ. In Hebrews 12:6,7 we read: "For whom the Lord loveth he chasteneth, and scourgeth every son whom he receiveth. If you endure chastening, God dealeth with you as with sons." God's hand of chastening on David was a hand of blessing. Its purpose was to keep David from falling into such sin again and to constantly remind him that what a man sows he also reaps.

The two leading themes in the Bible are sin and grace. Each is traced to its source. Sin is traced to Adam. Our inherited evil nature is from him. Grace is traced back to God and is part of His nature. Man by nature loves but it is a selfish love wanting everything for himself. It is a possessive and subjective love. God's love is objective. He offers everything He has for you and me and all others if we will but receive it.

In this sin of David's we see how vile the old nature in a man is, no matter if that man is a believer in Christ. In this incident we also see the grace of God and how God deals with man in grace. These two subjects are illustrated in the Bible time and again and exemplified in a number of persons. Between these two, sin on the one hand, and grace on the other, turn all the transactions between God and the souls of men.

The sin of man in all its hideousness is no more clearly revealed than in the case of David. He was a man after the heart of God, but he fell as low as any man could fall. The grace of God, however, worked such deep repentance that David found pardon and restoration. This was in contrast to Saul who in some respects seemed to be rejected for a milder offense. Actually, he rejected the grace of God which was the only means of his restoration.

God's grace leaves no room for presumptuous sinning. We need not think that because God forgave David, we may willfully sin and He will forgive us any time, any where, and restore us to fellowship and service. David knew the danger in this and prayed, "Keep back thy servant also from presumptuous sins; let them not have dominion over me" (Ps. 19:13). We dare not presume on the grace of God and seek to turn it into license. At the same time let us take heart, remembering that God who forgave David when he came clean, will also cleanse us from all unrighteousness if we as David confess our sins and come clean.

David rejoiced in the forgiveness of sins. He wrote: "Blessed is he whose transgression is forgiven, whose sin is covered. Blessed is the man unto whom the Lord imputeth not iniquity, and in whose spirit there is no guile" (Ps. 32:1,2).

Sometimes we think of this word "blessed" as being "happy," but if we do, we must not limit it to its usual meaning today, that of something frothy and light. The true happiness of a soul comes to the person whose sin is forgiven and removed and to whom the Lord does not impute iniquity. The record is clear. This was David's experience, for God had forgiven him. Sin was not imputed against his record so that he had to die for it.

As we saw in a previous portion of this study, as long as David kept silence his bones waxed old through his roaring all the day long. For a whole year he kept silence on his great sin, but his body was affected by it. He felt the hand of God heavy upon him night and day. This is evidence enough that he was still God's child—for whom the Lord loves He chastens and scourges every son He receives. David was dealt with as a son and felt the rod of God.

As long as David did not repent, God did not leave him in quietness and peace. Perhaps we have seen persons who keep on sinning and seem to have no trouble resulting from it either in their conscience or from others. This might well be a sign that they were never born of God. We have to be careful here, however, for we do not see the hearts of men. We may see a smiling face in public, yet that man or woman may have a very heavy heart in private. Then David said, "I have acknowledged my sin unto thee, and mine iniquity have I not hid. I said, I will confess my transgressions unto the Lord; and thou forgavest the iniquity of my sin." After that he commented on the sorrow that comes upon the wicked.

So then, if we are truly children of God and fall into sin, we will find God's hand heavy upon us. He will not let up until we come to Him with a broken and contrite heart. When we do, we will find forgiveness with Him. This is a most wonderful and satisfying truth.

David's sin had given the enemies of God great occasion to blaspheme. In addition, the child born of David's sin died. This raises two questions. Should a person be considered a Christian when he falls as low as David did? And why is it that a man must still suffer for the results of his sin after he has been forgiven?

Question One

Consider the first question: Can a person be considered a Christian when he falls as low in sin as David did? In Psalm 103:10 the Psalmist said, "He hath not dealt with us after our sins; nor rewarded us according to our iniquities." This simply means that God has not allowed all the judgment to fall on us that is really our due. If any of us received our just deserts, we would be cast into hell. God dealt with another concerning our sins and exacted from Him full satisfaction.

The payment of God cannot be demanded twice. Jesus Christ has already borne my sins; God will not exact the penal judgment a second time. Christ bore in His own body on the tree the result of our iniquities. When we accepted the Lord Jesus Christ as our personal Saviour, God, acting in His capacity as Judge, forgave us on the basis of Christ's merits. The penalty against us was annulled because the eternal consequences of sin were fully met in Christ, and this satisfied the justice of God. On the other hand, those who reject Christ turn away from the only source of salvation. Being spiritual bankrupts, they are lost and are without God and without hope in this world.

We learn in Romans 3:23, "All have sinned, and come short of the glory of God." This includes all of us. We are sinners by nature and practice. No man who has looked upon a woman with evil desire has any grounds for looking down upon David, for both are guilty of the same sin of adultery. Furthermore, the person who hates his brother is a murderer already. How many of us are better than David? If we were to receive what we deserved, we could never stand before God. Thank God, this is not all the Scripture has to tell us. Here is a glorious message: "Being justified freely by his grace through the redemption that is in Christ Jesus: To declare, I say, at this time, his righteousness: that he might be just, and the justifier of him which believeth in Jesus" (Rom. 3:24,26).

Question Two

We now consider the second question. If God really forgives, why must a man still suffer the result of his sin? Or, as some others might phrase it, "When God forgives, doesn't he forget?" What many want to know by such a question is, "If a man is forgiven of his sins and cleansed by the blood of Christ, do not all the consequences of sin vanish?" We have already answered this from the standpoint of God's chastening of His children which produces Christ-likeness in our lives.

Hebrews 12 is a key chapter in this respect. One of its

admonitions is, "Despise not thou the chastening of the Lord, nor faint when thou art rebuked of him: For whom the Lord loveth he chasteneth, and scourgeth every son whom he receiveth. If ye endure chastening, God dealeth with you as with sons: for what son is he whom the father chasteneth not?" Now, the chastening hand of the loving Father is a very different matter from the judgment of a Holy God. As the Moral Ruler of us who are believers, God deals with us governmentally. In forgiving us the eternal consequences of our sins in Christ, God has dealt with us judicially or from the standpoint of the Eternal Judge. But in chastening us and in allowing us to reap what we sow in this life even though we are believers, God is dealing with us governmentally.

A good illustration of this is found in the 11th chapter of I Corinthians. In verses 29 through 32 the Apostle Paul tells of some who were coming to the Lord's Supper and partaking of it in such a way as to bring condemnation to themselves. Here are the words: "For he that eateth and drinketh unworthily, eateth and drinketh damnation to himself [judgment or condemnation], not discerning the Lord's body. For this cause many are weak and sickly among you, and many sleep. For if we would judge [examine] ourselves, we should not be judged. But when we are judged [examined by God], we are chastened of the Lord, that we should not be condemned with the world."

God forgives His people, yet makes it very plain that He abhors sin. He teaches us to abhor sin by allowing us to taste the bitter fruit of it.

The Psalmist realized this, for he wrote in Psalm 99:8: "Thou answeredst them, O Lord our God: thou wast a God that forgavest them: though thou tookest vengeance of their inventions." The word "inventions" in this passage means "evil practices." Though God's people were forgiven of their sins, they still felt the consequences of those sins in their daily lives.

This is illustrated for us in Exodus 32. There we learn that the Children of Israel had Aaron make a golden calf for them which they worshipped. God moved to wipe them out, but Moses interceded for them. In answer to Moses' plea, "the Lord repented of the evil which he had thought to do unto the people." Though they were not all destroyed, they suffered the consequences of their idolatry, for we learn: "The Lord plagued the people, because they made the calf, which Aaron made."

Still another illustration of this truth is found in the experience of Moses and Aaron. These were good men, but toward the end of their earthly journey, they sinned in such a way that God said, "Because you believed me not, to sanctify me in the eyes of the children of Israel, therefore ye shall not bring this congregation into the land which I have given them" (Num. 20:12). This is repeated again concerning Aaron in verse 24: "Aaron shall be gathered unto his people: for he shall not enter into the land which I have given unto the children of Israel, because ye rebelled against my word at the water of Meribah." This was the time Aaron and Moses struck the rock instead of merely speaking to it as God had told them.

God forgave them completely, but for their good as His children, they were chastened by not being permitted to enter the land of Canaan. This was done so that those who came after them would recognize that God does not condone or overlook sin but always deals with it properly.

Consequently, while God pardoned David for his great sin, He still chastened him for his evil practices. David learned that the way of the transgressor is hard.

Sometimes these lessons have in them a bit of what men have termed "poetic justice." For example, Jacob deceived his father with the skin of a kid, so his sons deceived him by dipping Joseph's coat in the blood of a kid. Pharaoh cruelly ordered all of the boy babies born to the Israelites to be drowned. Later on, the fighting men of Egypt were drowned in the Red Sea. Nadab and Abihu, Aaron's sons, offered strange fire to the Lord, and were consumed by fire. Haman built a gallow for Mordecai, but he himself was hanged upon it.

These verses of Scripture take on new significance in the light of these illustrations. "Be not deceived, God is not mocked, for whatsoever a man soweth, that shall he also reap." "He that soweth to his flesh, shall of the flesh reap corruption, but he that soweth to the spirit, shall of the spirit reap life everlasting." Though the context of this verse which follows differs from these others, nevertheless, the principle it gives is in line with them: "He which soweth sparingly shall reap also sparingly; and he which soweth bountifully shall reap also bountifully. Every man shall receive his reward according to his own labour" (II Cor. 9:6; I Cor. 3:8).

God's purpose in dealing with us in such fashion is that we might learn not to sin. One cannot expect forgiveness and then be turned loose to go on living in the sin that brought God's displeasure. God fixed a gulf between sin and righteousness. This must be maintained. Absolutely no compromise is possible. No attempt should ever be made by us to reduce or detract from the absolute holiness and purity of God. Sin is always sin and righteousness is always righteousness. There is no blending of them in any way, shape or form. God cannot forgive us at the expense of lowering His standard of righteousness.

In order to teach us to hate sin, God brings His chastisement upon us. If He did not, we would be coming crawling to Him every five minutes for more pardon because of our continuing to live in sin. God's people are taught by Him to hate sin by its bitter consequences and are also brought through this to love righteousness or holiness. God chastens us as He pleases "for our profit, that we might be partakers of his holiness" (Heb. 12:10,11).

God does not want us to come to glory with nothing to show for our spiritual lives and service. He wants to see spiritual fruit and that in abundance.

CHAPTER SIXTEEN

DAVID'S SAD REAPING

II Samuel 12-18

When God forgives He at once restores. He never carries a grudge. Nevertheless, there are consequences that we must expect to face because of our sin. The Lord uses the rod of discipline on His children, apparently part of which is to let us reap what we sow. While He restores us to fellowship, the bitter cup which we have brewed for ourselves has to be drunk. David would live for 20 more years but the seeds of murder and lust that he had planted would bear fruit in his own family.

We have learned that God struck the child that Uriah's wife bare unto David "and it was very sick." On the seventh day the child died. This is a very sad story, and it covers a period of great searching of soul for David. During the seven days from the time that the child became ill until he died, David in great agony of heart pleaded for the child's life: "David therefore besought God for the child; and David fasted, and went in, and lay all night upon the earth. And the elders of his house arose, and went to him, to raise him up from the earth: but he would not, neither did he eat bread with them" (12:16,17).

The reason for David's conduct at this time is given in verses 22 and 23. "And he said, While the child was yet alive, I fasted and wept: for I said, Who can tell whether God will be gracious to me, that the child may live? But now he is dead, wherefore should I fast? can I bring him back again? I shall go to him, but he shall not return to me." These were the words of a man brokenhearted at the death of his son. The child was conceived out of wedlock but very possibly that which caused David's deepest suffering was seeing this innocent child passing through this illness because of his father's sin. This attitude indicates the true contrite spirit of this man.

In this David had learned one great lesson though he had many more to learn.

Another son was born to David and Bath-sheba and David "called his name Solomon: and the Lord loved him. And he sent by the hand of Nathan the prophet; and he called his name Jedidiah [beloved of the Lord], because of the Lord."

David and Bath-sheba's first son was taken from them because of their sin. But in the grace of God, this second son was chosen of God to succeed David on the throne.

Surely this is an indication of God's complete forgiveness of David and a fresh evidence of God's mercy. On the one hand we see the severity of God. On the other, we see His grace, since the lesson He taught His child had been learned.

Evil in David's House

God had also told David that He would raise up evil against him out of his own house. Part of this is seen in the disclosure in the sacred record of how David's son, Amnon, was guilty of sexually assaulting his half sister, Tamar. Here was a case where David's own son was manifesting the same kind of unbridled passion that David had expressed with Bath-sheba.

In the same 13th chapter of II Samuel, we learn how the third of David's sons, Absalom, the full brother of Tamar, waited for the opportune moment, then murdered Amnon in cold blood.

Like David's murder of Uriah, Absalom's murder of his half brother was premeditated. He called all the sons of David together for a feast and then commanded his servants: "Mark ye now when Amnon's heart is merry with wine, and when I say unto you, Smite Amnon; then kill him, fear not: have not I commanded you? be courageous, and be valiant. And the servants of Absalom did unto Amnon as Absalom had commanded."

Here again, the use of intoxicating liquors was employed. David had gotten Uriah drunk in the hope that he would go home to his wife and thus cover David's sin. Absalom got Amnon drunk so that he would not realize his danger until too late.

Absalom then fled to Talmai, the son of Ammihud, king of Geshur (13:37). He stayed there for three years and his father mourned for him every day of his absence.

The fact that Absalom went to Geshur, which was a heathen country, reminds us once again that David was reaping what he had sowed. Years before, in hiding from Saul, David had disobeyed the Lord by taking a wife, Maacah, daughter of the king of Geshur. Absalom was their son, and in him showed up the unprincipled character of his mother and the wild passions of his father.

In murdering Amnon, Absalom had also laid what he thought was the foundation for succeeding his father to the throne. In the natural course of things, the oldest son of a king would succeed to the throne at his father's death, but with Amnon dead, Absalom thought he stood much closer to the succession. He reckoned without God who had entirely different plans.

Absalom's Rebellion

Later, when Absalom returned to the kingdom, he stole the love of the people and rebelled against his father. The stage was set in an atmosphere of trickery and deceit. Absalom raised an army to depose his father, and David barely escaped with his life. It was following this that another part of the prophecy concerning the judgment on David's house was fulfilled. God had said that He would take David's wives and give them openly to his neighbor. When David fled, he left a number of his concubines behind to take care of his house. Ahithophel counseled Absalom: "Go in unto thy father's concubines, which he hath left to keep the house; and all Israel shall hear that thou art abhorred of thy father: then shall the hands of all that are with thee be strong. So they spread Absalom a tent upon the top of the house; and Absalom went in unto his father's concubines in the sight of all Israel. And the counsel of Ahithophel, which he counseled in those days, was as if a man had enquired at the oracle of God: so was all the counsel of Ahithophel both with David and with Absalom" (II Sam. 16:21-23).

David found that the way of the transgressor is hard and that what a man sows he reaps. Through his sins, David began a train of circumstances and events which, but for the grace of God, could have completely overwhelmed him.

It is very possible that David need not have fled Jerusalem. He might have stayed, mustered his men, and perhaps successfully have defended his kingdom at this time. But in the desire to spare his city and the innocent who would have suffered the most in such a situation, he fled. Some of the scenes which followed his exit from Jerusalem were heartbreaking. David believed his own sins were the root cause of this trouble, and he looked on Absalom's rebellion as God's chastening. David wept as he left his city. Such a man the Lord would not despise.

The writer of II Samuel tells us: "And David went up by the ascent of mount Olivet, and wept as he went up, and had his head covered, and he went barefoot: and all the people that was with him covered every man his head, and they went up, weeping as they went up" (15:30). Here is one of the real signs of contrition, of true repentance. This goes far beyond remorse. David was not weeping for the loss of his kingdom, but because of his own sins. He considered them to be the root cause of this civil strife.

As for ourselves, are not we too dry eyed today? We come to the close of a day and say, perhaps routinely: "Lord, if I have sinned against you this day, forgive me." Do we really face our sins in this way? Are we aware of God's chastisement upon us for sin? Chastisement is not judgment for sin, for our sins were all judged in Christ. Through chastisement we learn what sin is and that we should avoid it.

David's Six Hundred

David did not lack for men to follow him. The first group to stand with him were his 600 men who had joined him while he was in Gath. Some of them were foreigners who may have first come to David in unbelief; through his testimony, however, they apparently became believers. The reason for thinking this is that David said to Ittai, a leader among them: "Wherefore goest thou also with us? return to thy place, and abide with the king: for thou art a stranger, and also an exile. Whereas thou camest but yesterday, why should I this day make thee go up and down with us? seeing I go whither I may, return thou, and take back thy brethren: mercy and truth be with thee" (15:19,20). Why would David say, "Mercy and truth be with you" if they did not belong to the family of God?

Many of these men had been with David when he had suffered at the hands of Saul. They had witnessed the genuineness of David's faith and knew he was God's anointed. They believed God would someday establish him on the throne of Israel, and so they threw their lot in with him. They fought by his side, endured hunger, and had every opportunity to see the real David. Does our testimony ring true when trials come? Do others know by our reactions that we are genuine believers?

These men were experienced and tough warriors. David had organized them and trained them well. They threw in their lot with him when there was as yet no outward evidence he would ever be Israel's king. They had been his bodyguard for more than 20 years, but David was no longer a young man. It seemed for the time being that his cause was not popular; nevertheless, Ittai's answer to the king showed both devotion to David and to the Lord. His words were: "As the Lord liveth, and as my lord the king liveth, surely in what place my lord the king shall be, whether in death or life, even there also will thy servant be" (15:21).

These rugged soldiers had committed themselves to the king's cause while the lukewarm subjects of Israel chose Absalom's side when it looked at first that he would be successful. This is ever the case when great issues are at stake. There are those who look only for what seems to be popular rather than what is right. The true believer in Christ may be called on to suffer for the Lord's sake.

Have we followed Jesus in His rejection? The writer to the Hebrews gives us this admonition in chapter 13: "Wherefore Jesus also, that he might sanctify the people with his own blood, suffered without the gate. Let us go forth therefore unto him without the camp, bearing his reproach. For here have we no continuing city" (vv. 12-14).

We call ourselves Christians, the word Christian meaning "Christ's men." Are we? In order to be Christ's men, we must be willing to be sacrificed even unto death. Do we not read in Romans 12:1: "I beseech you therefore, brethren, by the mercies of God, that ye present your bodies a living sacrifice holy, acceptable unto God"? A living sacrifice is one that is dead to self but alive to God. This is in keeping with Matthew 10:39: "He that findeth his life shall lose it: and he that loseth his life for my sake shall find it." Along this same line Peter wrote: "The God of all grace, who hath called us unto his eternal glory by Christ Jesus, after that ye have suffered a while, make you perfect, stablish, strengthen, settle you." One other verse that encourages us in this difficult choice is, "And let us not be weary in well doing: for in due season we shall reap if we faint not" (Gal. 6:9). These principles were exemplified in the lives of these 600 men who were willing to give themselves totally and completely in life or in death to their rejected king. Let us heed their example and not be fair weather Christians, willing to follow Jesus only when things go well, but also in the times of difficulty and stress.

Will we take our stand with Ittai and say concerning our

Lord: "As the Lord liveth . . . whether in death or life, even there also will thy servant be"?

We dare not play fast and loose with that which belongs to God. Paul wrote to the Corinthians, "Know ye not that your bodies are the members of Christ?" (I Cor. 6:15). A few verses later on he stated: "What? know ye not that your body is the temple of the Holy Ghost which is in you, which ye have of God, and ye are not your own? For ye are bought with a price: therefore glorify God in your body, and in your spirit, which are God's" (vv. 19,20). Belshazzer, king of Babylon, took the vessels of gold and silver which had been dedicated to the Lord and used them for ungodly purposes. His judgment was swift. The handwriting on the wall marked the end of his kingdom. We belong to God. We have no right to use that which belongs to God for anything other than what He chooses. The path that Christ has marked off for us is the one we must follow. We are not our own. We are bought with a price.

Crossing Kidron

David was standing by the brook Kidron as he conversed with Ittai. When he saw the devotion of this man and his followers, he said to them, "Go and pass over." We also learned "all of the country wept with a loud voice, and all the people passed over: the king also himself passed over the brook Kidron, and all the people passed over, toward the way of the wilderness" (15:23). This stream or rivulet is located between the base of the temple hill and Mount Olivet in the valley of Moriah. Its functions were many. The sewage of the city was emptied into it and carried away. The blood from the sin offerings drained into it also. This has a typical significance in that it pictures the sin and iniquity of the people being washed away from before the face of Almighty God, whose Shekinah glory dwelt in the Holy of Holies.

In addition, the ashes of the idols that godly kings had destroyed were thrown into its waters and removed from the vicinity of Jerusalem.

Most significant of all was that our Saviour, the Lord Jesus Christ, passed over this brook on His way to Gethsemane just before He went to Calvary to bear our sins. Psalm 69, which speaks prophetically of our Saviour's suffering, tells of a prayer He uttered as He carried the load of sin on His heart: "Save me, O God; for the waters are come in unto my soul. I sink in deep mire, where there is no standing: I am come into deep waters, where the floods overflow me. I am weary of my crying: my throat is dried: mine eyes fail while I wait for my God." The imagery of these words was undoubtedly suggested by His passing through the mire and muck of this repulsive, nauseating stream, in those hours immediately preceding His death for us. Thus this rivulet speaks of the loathsomeness of sin and of the deep humility of our Saviour in dying for us.

This brook also stood associated with humiliation in the life of David. It represents the same for all his men who went with him outside the camp bearing His reproach. Have we followed Christ in this manner?

It was at this same place that Zadok the priest, having with him the ark of the covenant, met David. It is in this incident that the deep humility of David and his confidence in the wisdom of God stands out. "The king said unto Zadok, Carry back the ark of God into the city: if I shall find favour in the eyes of the Lord, he will bring me again, and show me both it, and his habitation: But if he thus say, I have no delight in thee; behold, here am I, let him do to me as seemeth good unto him" (15:25,26).

David did not feel himself worthy to have the ark with him. He reasoned, and rightly, that if his cause was God's cause, the Lord would permit David to return to Jerusalem and he would worship the Lord in the place God had established. If through God's mercy and power David returned, good and well; but under the uncertain conditions of that time David would not expose the ark. God had designated Jerusalem as the center of worship and David did not want to let the ups and downs of his career interfere with God's plans and possibly expose the ark to misuse. Once the clouds had cleared away and David was delivered, he sang: "He brought me forth also into a large place: he delivered me, because he delighted in me" (II Sam. 22:20). This does not mean God's delight was in David's merits, but God delighted in showing David mercy. It was the delight of love. God loved him and brought him back to his city and his throne.

It was as David crossed the brook Kidron, this place of rejection and humiliation, that he learned his best friend had deserted him. It was told David, saying, "Ahithophel is among the conspirators with Absalom. And David said, O Lord, I pray thee, turn the counsel of Ahithophel into foolishness."

Ahithophel had been David's counselor. It was of him David wrote in Psalm 55: "For it was not an enemy that reproached me; then I could have borne it: neither was it he that hated me that did magnify himself against me; then I would have hid myself from him: But it was thou, a man mine equal, my guide, and mine acquaintance. We took sweet counsel together, and walked into the house of God in company."

Ahithophel and David had been close friends. They talked over spiritual problems, of victories and of defeats. They discussed matters of state and went to the house of God together to inquire of the Lord which way they should turn. This man's wisdom had stood David in good stead time and again. Now Ahithophel had turned against him. The counselor deserted his king for Absalom, the usurper. This was hard for David to take and hard to understand. At a later time a greater David would suffer at the hands of Judas, one who had professed to be His friend, and yet who at the end turned against Him and betrayed Him to His enemies.

There was no excuse for Judas to turn against our Lord. Neither is there any excuse for us. With regard to Ahithophel and David, however, there could have been a reason. Ahithophel was the grandfather of Bath-sheba against whom David had so grievously sinned. Furthermore, Ahithophel's son was a friend and comrade of Uriah, Bath-sheba's husband. David's sin was such that Ahithophel could not forget it. He was deeply hurt. It is easy to understand why he would turn against David when this opportunity presented itself.

Are we willing to go outside the gate and bear the reproach of the Lord Jesus Christ? Are we willing to go into humiliation with Him? There is no other way—death and humiliation go before life and exaltation. This is what our Saviour was talking about when He said in John 12:23: "The hour is come, that the Son of man should be glorified. Verily, verily, I say unto you, Except a corn of wheat fall into the ground and die, it abideth alone: but if it die, it bringeth forth much fruit."

Preceding glorification and true life was death on the cross. The same principle of death before life holds in the spiritual realm. This is true not only of our salvation from the guilt of sin but it is also true in the believer's experience in salvation from the power of sin. In order to experience this wonderful life of His we will have to go with Him outside the camp, bearing His reproach.

Here are His own words: "He that loveth his life shall lose it; and he that hateth his life in this world shall keep it unto life eternal. If any man serve me, let him follow me; and where I am, there shall also my servant be: and if any man serve me, him will my Father honour" (John 12:25,26). In this connection Luke 9:23,24 is very important: "If any man will come after me [be my disciple], let him deny himself, and take up his cross daily, and follow me. For whosoever will save his life shall lose it: but whosoever shall lose his life for my sake, the same shall save it."

In contrast are these of whom John tells us in 12:42,43: "Nevertheless among the chief rulers also many believed on him; but because of the Pharisees they did not confess him, lest they should be put out of the synagogue: For they loved the praise of men more than the praise of God."

This is the spiritual significance of David's crossing the brook Kidron. He, so to speak, lost his life for the Lord's sake. The 600 men and the others who followed him lost their lives for David's sake and the Lord's sake—and all of them found it again. This is the way our Lord was exalted: "Let this mind be in you, which was also in Christ Jesus: Who, being in the form of God, thought it not robbery to be equal with God: But made himself of no reputation, and took upon him the form of a servant, and was made in the likeness of men: And being found in fashion as a man, he humbled himself, and became obedient unto death, even the death of the cross. Wherefore God also hath highly exalted him, and given him a name which is above every name: That at the name of Jesus every knee should bow, of things in heaven, and things in earth, and things under the earth; And every tongue should confess that Jesus Christ is Lord, to the glory of God the Father." Shall we go with Him outside the gate bearing His reproach? If we do, we will also have a part in His exaltation.

Footprints of Jesus

Sweetly, Lord, have we heard Thee calling, Come follow me!
And we see where Thy footprints falling Lead us to Thee.
Tho' they lead o'er the cold, dark mountains, Seeking His sheep;
Or along by Siloam's fountains, Helping the weak:
Footprints of Jesus, that make the pathway glow;
We will follow the steps of Jesus, where'er they go.
By and by, thro' the shining portals, Turning our feet,
We shall walk, with the glad immortals, Heav'ns golden street.

David Cursed by Shimei, II Samuel 16

One of David's most humiliating experiences during this retreat from Jerusalem was the verbal abuse heaped upon him by Shimei, a Benjamite, and a relative of Saul. The account in the Scripture is as follows: "And when king David came to Bahurim, behold, thence came out a man of the family of the house of Saul, whose name was Shimei, the son of Gera: he came forth, and cursed still as he came. And he cast stones at David, and at all the servants of king David: and all the people and all the mighty men were on his right hand and on his left. And thus said Shimei when he cursed, Come out, come out, thou bloody man, and thou man of Belial: The Lord hath returned upon thee all the blood of the house of Saul, in whose stead thou hast reigned; and the Lord hath delivered the kingdom into the hand of Absalom thy son: and, behold, thou art taken in thy mischief, because thou art a bloody man" (vv. 5-8).

Shimei's cursing of David and his accusations against him had no basis in fact. It was God who had exalted David to the throne, and of all the men of Israel, no one had been more careful than David himself to be free of the blood of any member of Saul's house. David's response is magnificent when we realize that he had his army with him and his personal bodyguard was at his side, composed of men whose deeds of valour were legendary among the Israelites.

One of David's three top men, Abishai, said to him, "Why should this dead dog curse my lord the king? let me go over, I pray thee, and take off his head. And the king said, What have I to do with you, ye sons of Zeruiah? so let him curse, because the Lord hath said unto him, Curse David. Who shall then say, Wherefore hast thou done so? And David said to Abishai, and to all his servants, Behold, my son, which came forth of my bowels, seeketh my life: how much more now may this Benjamite do it? let him alone, and let him curse; for the Lord hath bidden him. It may be that the Lord will look on mine affliction, and that the Lord will requite me good for his cursing this day" (vv. 9-12).

David still smarted under his terrible sin of several years back. He knew God had forgiven him. What he was suffering in fleeing from Jerusalem and from Absalom's evil purposes was not judgment but was permitted of God as chastening, so that David might be mellowed and might avoid falling into such sins again. Rather than strike the man down, David wanted to see the goodness of the Lord as a vindication of the falsehoods uttered by Shimei. So though this man continued to curse and to throw stones and dust at God's servants, David endured it.

What do we do when men falsely accuse us? Our natural impulse is to justify ourselves. It is only human to want to set things right. David, however, recognizing that God was permitting this, refused to take any action against Shimei. He had learned the truth that he so well expressed in Psalm 37:5, "Commit thy way unto the Lord; trust also in him; and he shall bring it to pass." This is exactly what David did in this instance. David also knew that God would bring forth His righteousness as the light and His judgment as the noonday (Ps. 37:6). We, too, may have to face slander and lying and cursing at times, but let God vindicate us. David accepted this situation knowing it was not the punishment of the judge but the chastisement of his Heavenly Father. He rested his case with the Lord.

It was during this time that he wrote Psalms 3 and 62. In Psalm 62 he said: "My soul, wait thou only upon God; for my expectation is from him. He only is my rock and my salvation: he is my defence; I shall not be moved. In God is my salvation and my glory: the rock of my strength, and my refuge, is in God. Trust in him at all times; ye people, pour out your heart before him: God is a refuge for us. Selah." That last word means that we are to think on these things. This was how David encouraged himself in the Lord, and we should follow his example.

God Rules Among Men

We have learned concerning Ahithophel that he was possibly the closest friend David had had and as a counselor there was none like him. "The counsel of Ahithophel, which he counselled in those days, was as if a man had enquired at the oracle of God: so was all the counsel of Ahithophel both with David and with Absalom." This man had the final word almost as though God spoke through him.

It was on Ahithophel's advice that Absalom defiled his father's concubines in the hopes that such base conduct would strengthen the hands of those who had joined Absalom's side. These men, however, had reckoned without God.

David sent a man named Hushai back to Jerusalem with the hope of getting him into Absalom's inner circle of counselors. David's purpose was that Hushai would be able to counteract the clever advice that he knew Ahithophel was capable of giving.

The scheme was evidently of the Lord, for when Ahithophel advised Absalom to take an army and go immediately after his father and his men and destroy them before they could gather their forces, Hushai counseled delay. He reminded Absalom that David and his men were men of war and that they were irritated in their minds as a bear robbed of her whelps. Hushai counseled caution lest Absalom's forces be given even slight reverses, reports of which might turn into the story of a major route and Absalom's cause suffer.

Absalom and his men said, "The counsel of Hushai the Archite is better than the counsel of Ahithophel. For the Lord had appointed to defeat the good counsel of Ahithophel, to the intent that the Lord might bring evil upon Absalom." God raises men or lowers them as He wills. Nebuchadnezzar learned this truth. God allowed madness to come upon him so that he lived like an animal in the field. His lesson was "to the intent that the living may know that the most High ruleth in the kingdom of men, and giveth it to whomsoever he will, and setteth up over it the basest of men" (Dan. 4:17).

Sometimes one nation is brought to prominence in order to punish another nation. Then that nation in turn is tested, and if necessary brought low. We, too, in our own country, cannot escape this principle in God's dealing with the nations. God may allow us to be brought under the judgment of the hand of evil men until we know that God rules in the heavens.

Death of Ahithophel and Absalom, II Samuel 17,18

In the 17th and 18th chapters of II Samuel we find the tide turning in favor of David. F. B. Meyer summarized this period of David's chastening in the following words: "Many were the afflictions of God's servant, but out of them all he was delivered. When he had learnt the lesson, the rod was stayed. He had been chastened with the rod of men and with the stripes of the children of men; but God did not take away His mercy from him as from Saul: his house, his throne, and kingdom, in spite of many conflicting forces, being made sure. Thus always—the rod, the stripes, the chastisement; but amid all the love of God, carrying out His redemptive purpose, never hasting, never resting, never forgetting, but making all things work together till the evil is eliminated, and the soul purged. Then the afterglow of blessing, the calm ending of the life of a serene sundown."

When the tide turned in David's favor, it turned fast. Ahithophel, whose defection cut David so deeply, was the first to go and that by his own hand. We already have seen that humanly speaking, Ahithophel had reason to be angry with David, but apparently David's genuine repentance had no effect on his counselor's attitude. It was due to David's brokenheartedness, that God spared him and delivered him at this time.

Ahithophel's counsel, had it been followed by Absalom, might have indeed proved disastrous for David and his cause. Hushai's advice was accepted in its place, and Ahithophel knew Absalom's cause was lost. "When Ahithophel saw that his counsel was not followed, he saddled his ass, and arose, and gat him home to his house, to his city, and put his household in order, and hanged himself, and died, and was buried in the sepulchre of his father" (II Sam. 17:23). He did not turn in repentance to God but turned and deliberately and premeditatedly planned death by his own hand. He tried to fix things up so that his family would not suffer as the result of his rebellion against the king. Ahithophel's sin had found him out, but unlike David, Ahithophel followed his own counsels and did not turn to the Lord for help.

Absalom's death was equally humiliating though caused by other means. He was a very conceited man, and had set up a pillar "which is in the king's dale: for he said, I have no son to keep my name in remembrance: and he called the pillar after his own name: and it is called unto this day, Absalom's place." It seems from this that he erected for himself a tombstone that would remind succeeding generations of him. They remembered him, but not in the manner he had hoped. He was not even buried in the place that he had prepared but in an unmarked grave except for a heap of stones, thus in a manner shameful to a man of his position and pretentions. We read, "And they took Absalom, and cast him into a great pit in the wood, and laid a very great heap of stones upon him: and all Israel fled every one to his tent." It was almost as if they had said here was a man who deserves stoning for his rebellion and we will cast stones upon him now. These were the only stones of remembrance that were laid for him.

Ahithophel and Absalom found out what Job had written many years before to the effect that the triumph of the wicked is short and that the joy of the hypocrite is but for a moment (Job 20:5). Their sin had found them out even as Moses had warned long before their day. What they did not find out was what David wrote in Psalm 16:11: "Thou wilt show me the path of life: in thy presence is fullness of joy; at thy right hand there are pleasures for evermore." The pleasures of sin are for a season, but the pleasures of God are for eternity. David had committed his way unto the Lord and God had brought it to pass.

David came to the point in his experience when he learned not to fear because he trusted the Lord so. He said in one place, while fleeing from Absalom, "I can lie down and sleep, for my peace resteth in him."

It was just because of such trust that God was able to bring forth David's righteousness as the light and his judgment as the noonday. David was completely vindicated, not that God overlooked his sin, but because he had come clean with sin, had confessed it, and accepted the chastisement of the Lord. Then it was that God could restore him and use him.

When David fled from Jerusalem, he had put his case in God's hands and decided that if God brought him back again safely that was good. If the Lord saw fit not to bring him back, that also was good, for such was God's mind. David's case did not rest on his own merits but in the love of God. What a difference between the man who sought everything for himself and the man who sought only the glory of God. Truly, he was a man after the heart of God!

Victory Through Grace

Conquering now and still to conquer,
Rideth a King in His might,
Leading the host of all the faithful
Into the midst of the fight;
See them with courage advancing,
Clad in their brilliant array,
Shouting the name of their Leader,
Hear them exultingly say:

Not to the strong is the battle,
Not to the swift is the race
Yet to the true and the faithful
Vict'ry is promised thro' grace.

Conquering now and still to conquer,
Jesus, Thou Ruler of all,
Thrones and their scepters all shall perish,
Crowns and their splendor shall fall,
Yet shall the armies Thou leadest,
Faithful and true to the last,
Find in Thy mansions eternal Rest,
When their warfare is past.

CHAPTER SEVENTEEN

BRING BACK THE KING

II Samuel 19

Only ten more years of life were left to David after the death of Absalom. Very little is said about them as compared to his earlier years, but what is recorded is for our learning and admonition.

With the deaths of Ahithophel and Absalom and the break up of Absalom's army, the rebellion fell to pieces. David, who had stayed in the desert east of Jordan, could have come right back to Jerusalem had he so desired. That would have been the natural thing to do. Any other person in his position might have gone back as quickly as possible, organized his armies, put down all opposition and have wasted no time in getting the reigns of government back in his hands. David was different. He was still the man after God's own heart, a man who waited on God and would only take that which God gave him.

We learn from verse 9: "And all the people were at strife throughout all the tribes of Israel, saying, The king saved us out of the hand of our enemies, and he delivered us out of the hand of the Philistines; and now he is fled out of the land for Absalom. And Absalom, whom we anointed over us, is dead in battle. Now therefore why speak ye not a word of bringing the king back?" For awhile some of them had followed the popular and glamorous figure of Absalom. They had foolishly thought that they would be better off under his leadership than under that of David's. The defeat of Absalom's army brought them to their senses. Why is it that so much of what we learn, we have to learn through hard and bitter experiences instead of simply believing God? At times we have offered a helping hand to young Christians whom we have seen going astray only to find out that they viewed life very much as we did at their age. This seems to be a characteristic of all of us that we have to learn much of what we have to learn by trial and error and sorrow and difficulty. Our own nation has a lesson in this that it will have to learn sooner or later. It is not always that which sounds good that is the best in the end.

Possibly all the tribes of Israel except Judah entered into this discussion among themselves. They recognized how good and able a ruler David had been, so they admonished each other to go and bring back the king.

Think of this from the standpoint of the Lord Jesus Christ. He is the One who saved us from our sins. He has promised to give us peace of mind and heart and to solve the heartaches and troubles we face and provide a way of escape in our times of testing. His offer is still good, but many of us run after the glamorous things of the world instead of looking to Him for our help. It is time that we came to our senses and brought the King back to rule in our hearts.

The Israelites had had many lessons along this very line, but they seemed to be a hard people to teach. Time and again we read something like this in the Book of Judges. "And the children of Israel did evil in the sight of the Lord, and served Baalim: And they forsook the Lord God of their fathers, which brought them out of the land of Egypt, and followed other gods, of the gods of the people that were round about them, and bowed themselves unto them, and provoked the Lord to anger. And they forsook the Lord . . . and the anger of the Lord was hot against Israel, and he delivered them into the hands of spoilers that spoiled them, and he sold them into the hands of their enemies round about, so that they could not any longer stand before their enemies" (Judg. 2:11-14). In some ways this is a parallel to our own situation where we worship the god of gold.

In His grace, the Lord "raised up judges, which delivered them [Israel] out of the hand of those that spoiled them. And when the Lord raised them up judges, then the Lord was with the judge, and delivered them out of the hand of their enemies all the days of the judge: for it repented the Lord because of their groanings by reason of them that oppressed them and vexed them. And it came to pass, when the judge was dead, that they returned, and corrupted themselves more than their fathers, in following other gods" (Judg. 2:16-19). This is the record of the Book of Judges, time and time again. Is our own spiritual record any better?

Nations have to be trained just as individuals have to be trained. God said, "I also will not henceforth drive out any from before them of the nations which Joshua left when he died: that through them I may prove Israel, whether they will keep the way of the Lord to walk therein, as their fathers did keep it, or not." Israel still was being tested in David's day and they had failed. The path of obedience for them then was to bring back their king.

How about ourselves? Have we been going after the world and the things of the world, with its comfort, and its money to where we have neglected our King?

Judah was quite remiss in the matter of bringing back the king, so David sent to Zadok and to Abiathar, the priests saying, "Speak unto the elders of Judah, saying, Why are ye the last to bring the king back to his house? Seeing the speech of all Israel is come to the king, even to his house. Ye are my brethren, ye are my bones, and my flesh: wherefore then are ye the last to bring back the king?" (vv. 11,12).

We expect those who do not know the Lord to be centered in the world and what it has to offer, but why should God's children become centered in its attractions? Prosperity in many cases has brought self-content. This is true of the church as a whole where we now seem to be in the Laodicean age whose chief characteristic is lukewarmness. Read what our Lord said in Revelation 3:15: "I know thy works, that thou art neither cold nor hot: I would thou wert cold or hot."

Cold, without doubt, refers to people who have never been born of God. He is speaking to a church which is not cold yet it is not hot either.

Take a look at the total Church of Jesus Christ today. There is much churchianity. Many churches are full and souls are being saved, but too many of the true believers have settled down to enjoy the world. The average believer is not deeply concerned about a world headed for hell. It is not deeply concerned about the possibility of God having to bring His judgment upon a nation which perhaps could at one time be considered Christian but is not now. Here is what God says: "So then because thou art lukewarm, and neither cold nor hot, I will spue thee out of my mouth. Because thou sayest, I am rich, and increased with goods, and have need of nothing; and knowest not that thou art wretched, and miserable, and poor, and blind, and naked." Actions speak louder than words; what we do indicates what we think. God's evaluation of this Laodicean church is that it is wretched, empty and naked.

Just as David admonished his own tribe for their tardiness in inviting him back, so God admonishes the Laodicean church to open its door and let Him come in. The Lord Jesus will not force His way in. He does not force Himself upon any man, but He is waiting for our invitation.

This verse which we so often apply to the unsaved is actually spoken to believers: "Behold, I stand at the door, and knock: and if any man hear my voice, and open the door, I will come in to him, and will sup with him, and he with me." The Lord Jesus is waiting for us to invite him to come back and have complete control in our hearts. He wants to reign as King within us. He gives this promise to the overcomer: "To him that overcometh will I grant to sit with me in my throne, even as I also overcame, and am set down with my Father in his throne." There is a time for us when we will either reign with Christ, or be refused reigning with Him depending on whether or not we have overcome in His strength.

David was finally brought back as king: "And he bowed

the heart of all the men of Judah . . . and they said, Return thou, and all thy servants, so the king returned." David was an overcomer in his day. Let us be overcomers in ours. This is possible only as we let Christ rule and reign in our hearts.

David's Careless Neglect, I Kings 1

David's last years possibly eight or nine after the death of Absalom were comparatively quiet. But there came a moment toward the last days of his life after he had reigned almost 40 years that a crisis was begun because he had been careless in making known his choice of a successor.

This crisis occurred when David was ill and about to die. His two oldest sons, Amnon and Absalom, were both dead, and a third son possibly died in his youth, for very little is known of him. The fourth son who was then David's oldest living son was Adonijah, the son of Haggith. He set himself up as king and prepared chariots and horsemen and 50 men to run before him. This man we are told had not been displeased by his father at any time. David had never said to him, "Why hast thou done so?"

This experience in David's life reminds us of a parallel situation in our own. The old flesh nature would like to rule as king within us, whereas now that we are saved, the Lord Jesus Christ should rule as King. According to Galatians 5:16 we are admonished to "Walk in the Spirit, and ye shall not fulfil the lust of the flesh." Adonijah is a good type of the old flesh, the old self-life. It says of this son of David that "he exalted himself." The flesh will always do that. This fallen nature within us, whatever our names may be, says to each of us, "I will be king."

That old "I" within us will always exalt itself unless we do something about it.

Adonijah, having exalted himself, gathered many people around him, though he was careful not to send his invitation to a few. He did not call upon such spiritual men as Zadok, Benaiah, and Nathan, the prophet. Neither, of course, did he invite Bath-sheba, or her son Solomon. Apparently those who were invited went gladly. There never seems to be a lack of company for those who want to follow the fleshy desires. The world is full of such.

A bit of Adonijah's character shows up in a conversation he had later on with Bath-sheba. In I Kings 2:15 we learn that he said, "Thou knowest that the kingdom was mine, and that all Israel set their faces on me, that I should reign." He is the center of his own attention as he says "mine," "me," and "I." This is always the attitude of the person who is dominated by his flesh nature.

In the same verse, however, Adonijah admits that the kingdom "is turned about, and is become my brother's: for it was his from the Lord." Though Adonijah did not like God's decision and was rebellious against it, he had to admit that it was God's will for Solomon and not for Adonijah to reign. He knew the will of God, but he did not want to obey it.

How like the old flesh this is again, because we learn that the flesh lusteth against the spirit, and the spirit against the flesh and these are contrary the one to the other, so that we cannot do the things that we would (Gal. 5:17). There is a constant conflict in the heart of every believer that can only be resolved by the choice he makes. Because a believer is born again of the Spirit of God and that Spirit has come into our lives to take control of our lives for the Lord Jesus Christ, we have One within us who opposes the flesh nature. This our fallen nature resents and opposes.

One writer has well said, "In every heart there is a throne and a cross. If Christ is on the throne, then self is on the cross. If self is on the throne, then Christ is still on the cross."

What were the factors that brought about Adonijah's attempt to take over the throne? There was only one, and that was neglect on David's part. He had not done what God had ordered him to do. It was carelessness, not rebellion; yet that carelessness opened the door for Satan's counterfeit. Our enemy is always looking for an opportunity to take over the control of our lives. Where he cannot stir us up to revolt against God, he will seek to make us careless in the things of

God, so that before we realize what is happening we are dominated by our fallen natures.

We must remember that Satan is ever seeking to take advantage of us in one way or another. The self-life is perhaps the strongest weapon he has to use. So we are warned to "be sober, be vigilant, because your adversary the devil, as a roaring lion, walketh about, seeking whom he may devour" (I Pet. 5:8).

Adonijah was not long left to his own devices. There were those in Israel who were looking to seeing the will of God done. Nathan the prophet came to Bath-sheba, the mother of Solomon, and urged her to go and tell David what was going on. It is always good to know that God never leaves us alone in our waywardness. There is always another force within us seeking to change the direction of our lives. Even though we become careless, the conviction of the Holy Spirit is brought to our hearts so that we are brought to the realization that self is reigning where God should be reigning. The Holy Spirit will not let us rest in our neglect or our stubborn self-seeking, whatever the case may be.

David the king did not know what Adonijah was doing, but ignorance was no excuse for him. The result could have been fatal for the kingdom and for Solomon.

Samson was ignorant that the power of God departed from him when he allowed Delilah to cut his hair. His ignorance was no excuse. In his case, it was fatal. He lost his power, he lost his vision, he lost his ministry; and though the Spirit of God gave him one more opportunity for service during that time, Samson lost his life.

The nation of Israel was also sinfully ignorant. They did not know the time of their visitation when Jesus Christ came and offered Himself to them. For some 2000 years they have, as a nation, been away from God.

No different is the church today as pictured in the Book of the Revelation. Concerning it the Lord has said, "Thou knowest not that thou art miserable, and blind, and naked." Ignorance is no excuse, and it can be fatal.

With the contest shaping up such as was taking place in Israel, a decision was called for on the part of David. His advisors told him that he was the one who could say whether Adonijah would rule or if Solomon would rule. David knew the Lord's mind on this subject, the problem was that he had neglected the matter. How like this is to our own heart and life. We are faced constantly with a decision of whether the fallen nature will reign within us or if we will let Christ reign. The spiritual lessons we learn from the Scriptures call upon us to make a choice. "Choose ye this day whom ye will serve." The choosing is ours, but once we make the choice, He will work out the problem to His glory and our good.

Indecision in a case like this is a terrible sin. David made up for his mistake of carelessness and made plain his choice. He declared to Bath-sheba: "Even as I sware unto thee by the Lord God of Israel, saying, Assuredly Solomon thy son shall reign after me . . . even so will I certainly do this day" (I Kings 1:30). Immediately, Nathan and Zadok and Benaiah were called in, and David instructed them to take Solomon, and put him on David's mule, anoint him, and blow the trumpet and say, "God save King Solomon" (v. 34).

Who sits upon the throne of our hearts? Is it self or is it Christ? A greater than Solomon has come to be our King. This one has bought us with a price. We belong to Him. We must put ourselves completely at His disposal. We are not called upon to be successful, but to be faithful. And faithfulness is His standard of success. Put Christ on the throne.

CHAPTER EIGHTEEN

SATAN'S LAST ATTACK UPON DAVID

II Samuel 24:1 and I Chronicles 21:1

This last attack of Satan upon David took place some 38 years after David had ascended the throne and about two years before his death. Satan was successful for a brief time in enticing David into sin, which should remind us that at no age are we free from being tested. At the same time we can have God's victory. Should we fall, we will find forgiveness and restoration if we are genuine in our repentance.

The two verses listed above may seem contradictory at first. Second Samuel 24:1 says, "And again the anger of the Lord was kindled against Israel, and he moved David against them to say, Go, number Israel and Judah." Then in I Chronicles 21:1 we learn: "And Satan stood up against Israel, and provoked David to number Israel." The word "provoke" in this passage means "enticed."

Satan had beguiled David into sinning on more than one occasion, yet the Devil could not keep him chained. There are two great expressions in David's Psalms that reveal his understanding of God's dealing with man. One is "the mercy of God" and the other has to do with "trusting God." These two expressions were very prominent in David's vocabulary as he told of his personal relationship with God. God never tempts any man to sin. When a man sins he is drawn away of his own lust and enticed. Consequently, we know that it was not God who lured David into doing something wrong at this time but Satan.

For a clearer understanding of what happened to David

at this time we should turn to the fifth and sixth chapters of Romans. The question is raised there: "Does the grace of God give liberty to sin?" Some would conclude that such is the case looking at the life of David. However, these studies we have conducted in the life of this man indicate the principles by which God works, and they prove that grace is not liberty or license to sin but a corrective for sin.

In view of these two Scriptures, some might think that David was free to do something wrong, then ask for mercy and to fall back into sin again and again. Some have taught that after reading Romans 5:19-21: "For as by one man's disobedience many were made sinners, so by the obedience of one shall many be made righteous. Moreover the law entered, that the offence might abound. But where sin abounded, grace did much more abound: That as sin hath reigned unto death, even so might grace reign through righteousness unto eternal life by Jesus Christ our Lord." These folk have said, "If grace abounds because sin abounds, why not just go ahead and sin, which will make God's grace abound just that much more?" This is the very position that Paul refutes when he says in chapter six of Romans: "What shall we say then? Shall we continue in sin, that grace may abound? God forbid. How shall we that are dead in sin, live any longer therein?" (vv. 1,2).

Now, if any of us think that God has given freedom for us to sin and that He did so in David's life, we are being presumptuous. No such conclusion can be reached from an honest look at the facts.

David speaks of presumptuous sin in Psalm 19:13 where he prays, "Keep back thy servant also from presumptuous sins; let them not have dominion over me." David might have decided that since God had forgiven him this sin and that sin and that he fell so deeply into one sin after another, that one more sin would not matter very much. But it was from this very thing David wanted to be kept. He did not want such an idea to have dominion over him. The reason is given in the following words: "Then shall I be upright, and I shall be innocent from the great transgression." The Scriptures tell us that there is a sin unto death and this is a sin which a Christian can commit. This is a sin where we presume on God's grace and think that no matter what we do God will forgive us and clear the record. That is the sin of presumption which leads to the sin unto death. The sin unto death is one committed by a Christian which makes it necessary for God to call him home before his work and service are completed. John warns of this in his first epistle (I John 5:16).

In the incident before us with regard to David, we found that God was displeased with Israel for their continued sinning and knew that the nation as a whole needed the discipline of judgment. It is apparent also that David was becoming less watchful in his own spiritual life, and so God allowed Satan (as He did in the life of Job) to test the nation through their king. The Scriptures tell us "Satan stood up against Israel, and provoked David to number Israel." It has already been pointed out that the word "provoke" means "enticed" in this context. It was David then, who bore the brunt of this test and yet there was a moral link with the whole nation involved.

Satan's animosity is against Christ and the Holy Spirit; consequently, the man who seeks to practice the indwelling Christ becomes a victim of Satan's attacks. It is part of Satan's strategy not to center his attention on many believers if he can undermine the spiritual life of key Christian leaders. Perhaps it is a missionary, or a leader of some organization, or a pastor, or an evangelist. Such leaders must ever be on guard and watch and pray as the Scriptures enjoin. But every believer ought to be standing by those in positions of Christian leadership. The tendency is to criticize rather than to uphold them in prayer. This in itself will bring God's chastisement. Satan's strategy with Israel was to tempt David and through him the nation.

Ordinarily one could see nothing wrong with numbering a people. Census taking is done periodically by any alert government. But the numbering of the children of Israel was a matter of pride. David wanted to know how strong his nation was militarily. His strength really lay in God, but David laid his emphasis upon his armies. God's position was, "You do not need to number the people. I have taken care of this situation." The strength of Israel's army meant nothing if God was not with them to give them the victory.

The same is true with us in our spiritual life. Until we come to the place where each one of us says with true conviction, "I am nothing," God cannot do much for us. He has chosen that which is nothing to confound the wisdom of the wise. Our sufficiency is of God, not of ourselves.

God was displeased with this census which was rooted in pride and the glorification of man power and He "smote all Israel." David was awakened to his own folly in this and said to God, "I have sinned greatly because I have done this thing. But now, I beseech thee, do away with the iniquity of thy servant, for I have done foolish things." David again repents. He had not sinned presumptuously. He had been caught off guard once again by the Evil One. David had not lacked warning before he made the census, for Joab, a man that could not be called a godly man, reproved him, and his elders also protested. But David stubbornly insisted on going ahead to find out how strong his nation was. Not until God's displeasure was seen did David awaken to his sin.

When David repented, the Lord sent Gad with a message saying, "Go and say unto David, Thus saith the Lord, I offer thee three things; choose thee one of them, that I may do it unto thee." This was putting the choice of punishment up to David, and these choices according to I Chronicles 21:22 were: "Either three years' famine; or three months to be destroyed before thy foes, or else three days . . . even the pestilence in the land."

The choice was David's. He knew something of man, for he had learned something of the deceitfulness of his own heart. He had seen through the years how he, himself, responded when his fallen nature was in control. He must have reasoned that if he, as a man of God, could fall as low as he had fallen, it would be terrible for him to fall into the hands of ungodly men who had no respect for God whatsoever. David had learned something else throughout those years. He had come to know God personally and this knowledge had transformed his life. It was because of this background of knowledge that David said to Gad, "I am in a great strait: let us fall now into the hand of the Lord; for his mercies are great: and let me not fall into the hand of man." David chose to put his case in the hands of God who is all merciful.

David learned again that no man lives to himself and no man dies to himself. One person's sins can bring trouble to others. In this case, however, Israel was not faultless and the "Lord sent a pestilence upon Israel . . . and there died of the people seventy thousand men" (II Sam. 24:15). David had numbered the men available for warfare and found out there were over one million of them. This pestilence, which lasted for only a few days, showed David that if God so desired, He could make these men as nothing. God let David know, and the world and Israel know, that no man and no nation have any reason to boast of their strength. In a moment they can be taken as were those seventy thousand men who died of the pestilence in Israel.

David had also had the chance to see the angel with the drawn sword who was on his way to Jerusalem to strike the people there with pestilence. But David spoke before the Lord and pleaded for the life of the people in Jerusalem saying, "Is it not I that commanded the people to be numbered? even I it is that have sinned and done evil indeed; but as for these sheep, what have they done? let thine hand, I pray thee, O Lord my God, be on me, and on my father's house; but not on thy people, that they should be plagued" (I Chron. 21:17). In this David reveals the true condition of his heart. He did not take satisfaction in the fact that he had escaped the plague, though that might have been the reaction of some of us. When David saw this as his sin, he confessed his fault and pleaded on behalf of his people.

The Lord not only stayed the plague, but through God

He also instructed David to build an altar to the Lord on the threshing floor of Ornan, the Jebusite (I Chron. 21:18). The Lord was very specific about this and left no alternative in the matter. Why this particular spot should be chosen does not appear in the narrative, but later on in II Chronicles 3:1 we have this statement: "Then Solomon began to build the house of the Lord at Jerusalem in mount Moriah, where the Lord appeared unto David his father, in the place that David had prepared in the threshingfloor of Ornan the Jebusite."

Mount Moriah is significant in Bible history. It was the place where Abraham brought Isaac to offer him as a sacrifice to God. Later it became the site for the temple and the place where the temple sacrifices were brought.

It is interesting to see Ornan's reaction when he saw David and his men and heard David's proposition. He offered it to David free and also promised to furnish all the animals that David would need for an offering. This, David refused and stated a very important principle in doing so: "And king David said to Ornan, Nay; but I will verily buy it for the full price: for I will not take that which is thine for the Lord, nor offer burnt-offerings without cost" (I Chron. 21:24).

Had David been a grasping, selfish man, he might have looked on this as an opportunity to fulfill the will of God without any cost to himself. He had been passed over when the plague struck men in Israel and now a rich man had offered him a threshingfloor for an altar, and animals and grain for the offerings. But David refused to bring before the Lord that which cost him nothing. It may help clarify David's expression in this situation to see how it is stated in II Samuel 24:24: "And the king said unto Araunah [Ornan], Nay; but I will surely buy it of thee at a price: neither will I offer burnt-offerings unto the Lord my God of that which doth cost me nothing."

David paid full price for the threshingfloor and the surrounding land. He then built an altar on the threshingfloor itself and offered both burnt and peace offerings to God. Then a remarkable thing took place. David called on the Lord and the Lord "answered him from heaven by fire upon the altar of burnt-offering" (I Chron. 21:26). Sometimes we think that the only time God consumed an offering by fire from heaven was at the time when Elijah had his contest with the prophets of Baal. But it is very probable that this was the very method God used to show His approval of Abel's offering over against that of Cain's.

The fact that God sent fire to burn up the offering is very important in Scripture. Fire represents the wrath of God upon sin, a wrath which only He can exercise upon our sin. We cannot pay for our own sin. This must be done by God. From Isaiah we learn concerning Christ that "For the transgression of my people was he stricken" (Isa. 53:8). The way Paul states it in Romans 4:25 is, "Who was delivered for our offences, and was raised again for our justification." God's wrath on sin was exercised against the Lord Jesus Christ, our Saviour.

To those who will not receive Christ, with whom God is satisfied as having borne His wrath against sin, there is only the judgment of wrath and it is a fiery judgment that is predicted. In writing to the Thessalonians Paul said, "And to you who are troubled rest with us, when the Lord Jesus shall be revealed from heaven with his mighty angels, In flaming fire taking vengeance on them that know not God, and that obey not the gospel of our Lord Jesus Christ: Who shall be punished with everlasting destruction from the presence of the Lord, and from the glory of his power; When he shall come to be glorified in his saints" (II Thess. 1:7-10).

God's wrath for sin was spent on Christ for all who will receive Him as Saviour. Such will never face judgment again. But for those who will not accept God's offer of salvation through Christ, there is no alternative. God's wrath upon sin is by fire.

CHAPTER NINETEEN

DAVID HANDS ON THE TORCH

II Samuel 7 and I Chronicles 22

David was king of Israel for 40 years. Many of those years had been troublesome, but now, at the end of his life with his work about over, David had time to survey his work. How much of it was permanent? How much of it was really vital? How much of it had been spiritually effective before God? David had to give an account before God of his stewardship as a king. The time will come for us, perhaps sooner than we think, to give an account of our stewardship: "For we must all appear before the judgment seat of Christ; that every one may receive the things done in his body, according to that he hath done, whether it be good or bad" (II Cor. 5:10).

The greatest ambition in David's life was to build a house for God. This is ground covered in a previous chapter, but review at this point will be beneficial. "And it came to pass, when the king sat in his house, and the Lord had given him rest round about from all his enemies; That the king said unto Nathan the prophet, See now, I dwell in a house of cedar, but the ark of God dwelleth within curtains. And Nathan said to the king, Go, do all that is in thine heart; for the Lord is with thee" (II Sam. 7). This incident took place 25 years before David was called into the presence of God. But David's ambition was not realized. Though David had Nathan's blessing, he did not have God's blessing. That very night God told Nathan that David was not to build a house for Him. God's promise was that David would have a son who would fulfill that ambition and that God would establish that son's kingdom. "He shall build a house for my name, and I will stablish the throne of his kingdom for ever" (II Sam. 7).

What did David do in the face of God's refusal to realize his ambition? Did he become sour? Did he become resigned to fate, so to speak, and just give up? Did he feel frustrated and turn away from giving any attention to God's work at all? What would our reactions have been if our most holy ambitions for our God were denied us?

David serves as a good example for us. He gave himself even more diligently to serving the Lord. Is this our attitude? The whole matter can be summarized in this simple question: "Whose glory do we want? our's or God's?" David's answer to this is shown in his attitude and his actions. God was first in his life.

How would we react to being taken from the spotlight of publicity and placed in obscurity? What would be our reaction if we were removed by God from what looked like a situation of success and placed in one that looked like failure? What is our reaction when our early dreams of doing great things for God are suddenly shattered? Will we step out of the service of God or will we do as David did and behind the scenes prepare the materials for our successor to use?

Some, in the early enthusiasm of their youth and devotion to Christ, have dreams of doing great things for the Lord. They see themselves filling positions of influence, organizing and carrying on what the world considers a great task for God. Then we begin to realize that our work will be small, much of it done in obscurity. What then?

Perhaps as church members we have had some small success in the organizational work of the local church. Perhaps we have served as Sunday school superintendent or as head of one of the societies in the church, but only for a brief time. Someone else has taken over the responsibility and perhaps have even been honored for something that we did. What is our attitude? When faced with such a situation let us ask ourselves, "Am I seeking my own honor or God's honor?"

David took God's "No" in good heart and did what he could to insure the building of the temple, though he, himself, was to have no part in its actual erection. After the remarkable display of God's approval of the sacrifice David had offered on the threshingfloor of Araunah David said, "This is the house of the Lord God, and this is the altar of the burnt-offering for Israel. And David commanded to gather together the strangers that were in the land of Israel; and he set masons to hew wrought stones to build the house of God. And David prepared iron in abundance for the nails for the doors of the gates, and for the joinings; and brass in abundance without weight; Also cedar trees in abundance: for the Zidonians and they of Tyre brought much cedar wood to David" (I Chron. 22:1-4). In this manner David set about getting things ready for the day they would be needed for the temple.

David also said, "Solomon my son is young and tender, and the house that is to be builded for the Lord must be exceeding magnifical, of fame and of glory throughout all countries: I will therefore now make preparation for it. So David prepared abundantly before his death" (I Chron. 22:5). David intended this to be the most costly and magnificent building ever built. He wanted the fame and the glory of it to be known throughout the world so that people would come to see it and in this way come to learn of the true God. Such a building would bring fame to the man who built it, but the primary purpose of the building itself was to bring honor and glory to God.

Israel had been set in the midst of the nations to be a shining light. The heathen living in idolatrous darkness would look to this center and learn the truth of God. It was God's name David wanted honored, not his own or that of his son.

In verse 14 of I Chronicles 22 we find David saying, "Now, behold, in my trouble I have prepared for the house of the Lord a hundred thousand talents of gold, and a thousand thousand talents of silver; and of brass and iron without weight; for it is in abundance: timber also and stone have I prepared; and thou mayest add thereto." This was not done in peace and quiet but in the midst of a busy life and often a troubled life. There was opposition from the outside. There was the constant battle with sin in his own heart. A lesser man than David might have given up, but David appropriated the mercies of God and the grace of God for both his present and his future. Though God had said "No" to him with regard to building a temple, he did not slack his interest a moment in the glory of God. David set himself to do what he could to prepare for that building which God had promised Solomon would build. It made no difference to David that the honor of being the builder would go to Solomon. All David was concerned about was that God's glory would be the end result.

David had undoubtedly gathered together many spoils from his wars of conquest. Today's value on the gold he gathered would be something like three billion dollars. There was also some two billion dollars worth of silver besides brass, iron, timber and stone without measure.

David not only gave out of his surplus, but he also gave out of his own living for the house of the Lord. He said, "Moreover, because I have set my affection to the house of my God, I have of mine own proper good, of gold and silver, which I have given to the house of my God, over and above all that I have prepared for the holy house, Even three thousand talents of gold." In other words, out of the money that David was apportioned for his expenses such as the upkeep of his home, he gave 87 million dollars worth of gold, 12 and one-half million dollars worth of silver.

Then he called upon his people to give. They contributed another 145 million dollars worth of gold and 20 million dollars worth of silver. This was not a tax laid upon them, but an offering they gave freely. "Then the people rejoiced, for that they offered willingly, because with perfect heart they offered willingly to the Lord: and David the king also rejoiced with great joy."

All of this was given for a material building that God might call His special dwelling place here upon the earth. Now God does not dwell in temples made with hands. He lives in the believers. We are the temple of God today. "Know ye not that your body is the temple of the Holy Ghost which is in you, which ye have of God, and ye are not your own? For ye are bought with a price." Who can place a value on what it cost to redeem just one of us. The materials alone that went into Solomon's temple were worth billions of dollars; but who can put a price on the precious blood of the Lord Jesus Christ that was shed for us? There can be no comparison in cost and there is no comparison in glory either. Let us surrender ourselves entirely to God, regardless of what anyone else may think, or regardless of who may get the glory for what we do.

CHAPTER TWENTY

DAVID THE MAN AFTER GOD'S OWN HEART

In this final chapter we want to summarize the factors which showed David to be a man after the heart of God. Here, however, is no mere repetition of matters already covered. We dig a little deeper into the treasure of the Word and find more gems of truth to add to our spiritual wealth.

About ten years before David was born, God said to Saul, through Samuel the prophet: "Thy kingdom shall not continue: the Lord hath sought him a man after his own heart, and the Lord hath commanded him to be captain over his people, because thou hast not kept that which the Lord commanded thee" (I Sam. 13:14). We are not left to guess what the expression "a man after his own heart" means. In addressing the Jews in the synagogue at Antioch, Paul provided the definition: "And when he had removed him [Saul], he raised up unto them David to be their king; to whom also he gave testimony, and said, I have found David the son of Jesse, a man after mine own heart, which shall fulfil all my will" (Acts 13:22). There is the key—WHICH SHALL FULFIL ALL MY WILL.

In the heart of the Christian who is devoted to the Lord, there is the yearning to please Him. But how can this be done? A clue is provided in Psalm 89:20 where we read, "I have found David my servant; with my holy oil have I anointed him." The word "servant" here is significant. It means "a doer, a tiller of the soil, a slave, a bondsman." This in essence is what David was to God. He was God's bondsman doing whatever God required of him.

Outward obedience by itself, however, does not produce a man after the heart of God. A man under law might obey for fear of the consequences, but something more is needed to please God. Preceding obedience there must be the factor of faith. We do not gladly obey someone we do not believe in or trust. We must have a true conception and knowledge of God if we are to obey Him. That was the key to David's obedience.

We read concerning Enoch in Hebrews 11:5,6: "By faith Enoch was translated that he should not see death . . . he had this testimony, that he pleased God. But without faith it is impossible to please him: for he that cometh to God must believe that he is, and that he is a rewarder of them that diligently seek him." Thus it is clear that genuine faith in God precedes obedience, because without faith we cannot please Him.

We must consider this matter a little more closely, however, because most people will say, "I believe there is a God." But to some He is "the man upstairs." To some others, He is a Being greater and higher than man. To some of us He is the God who controls the universe, but He is not the God who controls our lives. To some of us He is the God who in mighty power provided the Lord Jesus Christ as Saviour and through Him saved us; but does He have our complete and willing obedience? We are not really believing in God in the Bible sense unless He is all in all to us and has all of us. God is a rewarder of them that diligently seek Him, which means more than going through the form of devotional periods. It means wanting above all else to have His will done in our lives. We want Him to be pleased in us.

The 11th chapter of Hebrews says, concerning hearers of the faith including David, "What shall I more say? for the time would fail me to tell of Gedeon, and of Barak, and of Samson, and of Jephthae; of David also, and Samuel, and of the prophets: Who through faith subdued kingdoms, wrought righteousness, obtained promises, stopped the mouths of lions . . . who in weakness were made strong, who waxed valiant in fight, turned to flight the armies of the aliens" (vv. 32-34). This was the kind of man David was through faith.

Faith and obedience are not synonymous terms, yet we cannot separate them, for they complement each other so closely. James makes this very clear when he says, "Seest thou how faith wrought with his works, and by works was faith made perfect?" (2:22). This was said of Abraham, but it could be said of other believers like Abraham. In David, too, his faith resulted in works. And through his works his faith was made more complete.

There is still another factor to be considered with regard to obedience. Not only is there faith that precedes obedience, but there also is a heart attitude of humility which is directly connected to faith and obedience. This was what Samuel learned when he looked for a man to take the place of Saul. He met Eliab and thought in his heart that he must be the man God would have for Saul's successor. The Lord corrected him by saying, "Look not at his countenance, or at the height of his stature, because I have refused him, for the Lord seeth not as man seeth for man looketh on the outward appearance, but the Lord looketh on the heart."

Knowing this will help us to understand why David, in spite of his failures, could still be a man after the heart of God. In spite of all his shortcomings, and his sin, David's heart attitude was such that God could deal with him and bring him to a place of repentance, restore him to fellowship, and work through him again. This was only possible because David's heart was basically right with God. David learned to have no confidence in the flesh. At the same time by the grace of God he learned through these failures to trust God and to give Him complete control in his life.

These three words must be kept before us as we consider what made David a man after the heart of God. Faith was basic to his life, his heart attitude was that of deep humility, and there was obedience. His humility caused him to realize that in himself he was nothing. Only through God could he perform the will of God. He put himself at God's disposal so that God could work His will through him.

We must constantly keep before us the principle Paul laid down in I Corinthians 1 with regard to those who are called of God. Not many wise men after the flesh, not many mighty, not many noble are called. God has chosen the foolish things of the world to confound the wise and the weak things of the world to confound the mighty. It is the thing that the world despises that God has chosen, yes, and the things that are not, to bring to nothing the things that are. Faith without humility would not lead to true obedience.

David demonstrated his humility in a number of ways. We saw in the early part of the study of David's life that though he was crowned to be king, he did not assert his rights in any way but subjected himself completely to the very man whom God had rejected. This was true humility. He did as our Lord admonishes us to do in Luke 9:23. David "denied himself" and took up his cross and followed his God. David's knowledge of God had been tested and his faith in God had been proved while he was still a young lad herding sheep. When bears and lions came to destroy his flock, David through his faith in God and with power provided by God overcame these ferocious beasts.

David's courage was based on his knowledge of God. He had an unspoiled reverence for God. His zeal was the result of his personal and close fellowship with his Lord. David learned in his day the truth that Paul expressed when he stated in Philippians 3:10: "That I might know him, and the power of his resurrection."

He believed that no man was strong enough to defy God. Consequently, when he heard the boasts of Goliath, David's zeal for God came to the surface. He, when chided by his brother, demanded of him, "Is there not a cause?" His faith and his works went together, neither of which would have been in evidence had he been haughty and self-asserting. In slaying Goliath we see in David faith, humility, courage, and of course, obedience to God. God could have destroyed Goliath without the help of man, but God has chosen to work through men who humble themselves before Him and are willing instruments to fulfill His will.

David had learned what it meant to commit his way unto the Lord, to trust in Him and see Him bring it to pass.

As we do as David did, we find that "though we walk in the flesh, we do not war after the flesh: (For the weapons of our warfare are not carnal, but mighty through God to the pulling down of strong holds;) Casting down imaginations, and every high thing that exalteth itself against the knowledge of God, and bringing into captivity every thought to the obedience of Christ" (II Cor. 10:3-5). This was how David lived. He believed in God's almighty power, trusted in God, and allowed God to use him. He did things that were impossible to mere human power alone, because he remembered that the battle was the Lord's and not his. This is the kind of man God is looking for today: "For the eyes of the Lord run to and fro throughout the whole earth, to show himself strong in the behalf of them whose heart is perfect toward him" (II Chron. 16:9).

There were aspects of David's life so much a picture of Christ that many of the Psalms written out of David's deep experiences are also prophetic utterences concerning Christ himself. Again and again we see Christ's life portrayed in these inspired hymns.

The attitude of mind that characterized our Lord is given in Philippians 2:6-8: "Who, being in the form of God, thought it not robbery to be equal with God: But made himself of no reputation, and took upon him the form of a servant, and was made in the likeness of men: And being found in fashion as a man, he humbled himself, and became obedient unto death, even the death of the cross." Our Lord did not seek His own will, but the will of the Father.

Though Christ was a member of the Godhead, He did not assert the rights of deity when He came to this earth but humbled Himself. David reflected this in his own life in that though he rightly was king, he did not assume those rights. In the face of popularity he had the heart attitude of humility. Though he was considered a public hero, wherever he was sent he "behaved himself wisely." He was loved by Michal, the king's daughter, and held in respect by the enemies of his nation. Yet, in all of this he conducted himself wisely. David's whole attitude was that God was going to make him king. This would be God's doings, and David determined to wait God's time.

The word "wait" is another important word to add to our vocabulary when we study the life of David. In contrast to his waiting, we find a great deal of impatience today and running ahead of God. The Lord Jesus said, "Follow me and I will make you fishers of men," but such following implies waiting upon Him. David's humility did not stand alone since it was rooted in faith. It produced following and waiting. David was content to let the Lord set the time when he was to come to the throne. The time, the place, the circumstances of David's coronation day were in the hands of his God. He did not run ahead of God's will in these matters.

David did not seek his own rights even under persecution. He constantly demonstrated humility in the face of impending death. In the main, he showed a calm and quiet heart before the Lord and before his adversaries. He cast his case upon the Lord because he found that God was his Strength and his Defense. This, as we have seen, was his testimony in Psalm 59. "Yea," he said, "I will sing aloud of thy mercy in the morning: for thou hast been my defence and my refuge in the day of my trouble . . . for God is my defence, and the God of my mercy." This is said for us in different words in Ephesians 6 where we are told to be strong in the Lord and in the power of His might and to put on the whole armor of God. God is our defense, also.

David prayed himself out of panic, out of fear, and out of doubt into perfect confidence and joyful song. Faith is the substance of things hoped for, the evidence of things not seen. This was David's experience and it can be ours.

David's song of victory did not always arise out of a change of circumstances. Often the circumstances continued and his cry of deliverance became calm waiting upon God. Too many of us pray but do not wait. Twice David had the opportunity to take the life of Saul, and humanly speaking, David's fugitive days might then have ended. But David's times were in God's hands, and that is where he left them. He wanted God to have the preeminence and the honor of completely controlling his life and future.

Waiting on God during the testing times of God can also be God's will for us.

David was not a hearer of the Word of God only, but a doer. He did not only want to know the Lord's will for the sake of knowing it, but for the purpose of doing it. What are we doing about God's will? Are we seeking it? and are we doing it, when we find it?

A guided life is a life dependent upon a cleansed heart. This is clear from Psalm 25. Even after the death of Saul David waited and sought the will of God. David was first given rulership over Judah, but he had to wait for years before the northern tribes were ready to receive him. That waiting period proved to be God's will for him. David was content to let God call the signals in his life.

David's Attitude in Face of His Failure and Defeats

David's lessons were learned at times through hard trials and even his defeats. When he left Israel and lived in Ziklag, he suffered from having gone to the enemy instead of resting his case with God. But through all this time his conscience was sensitive and was sharpened by the series of failures and defeats he experienced in those months. David learned there was no good thing dwelling in his flesh, that he, as others, was totally depraved. He learned that if he depended upon his own thinking and desires he would end up a failure. He was soon sick and tired of it all. The problem with many of us is that we do not become tired of our failures. We seem to love them; at least our actions suggest such is the case.

It was when David came to the end of himself, when there was no human device that he could think of for deliverance, that he turned to God. He cast himself upon God's mercy and grace. He became a brokenhearted man with a contrite spirit before God. He saw himself as God saw him, but he also saw God as He is, and he found that God did not despise him.

See also David's attitude as he faced his own sins. He was not a man after God's own heart because he was sinless or faultless. He was a man after the heart of God because he wanted to do the will of God. When convicted of his faults and sins, some of which were very great, he faced them. He did not dodge them. So often we pass off our sins lightly saying perhaps at the end of the day: "If I have failed today or if I have sinned, please forgive me."

God expects us to face sin as David faced sin. This will be the case if we allow the Holy Spirit to control us. There is no point in our trying to evade our sins when God brings them before us. We must not dodge them or make excuses for them as did Adam and Eve, but face them as God presents them to us.

David acknowledged God's great hatred for sin. When we stop to consider that God is pure and holy, we begin to realize how much He abhors sin. Might well we wonder how He can love us when we continue in sin.

David also acknowledged God's right to judge sin; and when God chastised him, he said God had a right to do so.

He always sought out God's mercy, for it was only on the basis of mercy that David could be forgiven and restored. In Psalm 103 he said, "He hath not dealt with us after our sins; nor rewarded us according to our iniquities" (v. 10). David acknowledged that he deserved more in the way of chastisement than he received.

Looking at God's mercy, he said, "For as the heaven is high above the earth, so great is his mercy toward them that fear him. As far as the east is from the west, so far hath he removed our transgressions from us. Like as a father pitieth his children, so the Lord pitieth them that fear him. For he knoweth our frame; he remembereth that we are dust" (vv. 11-14).

God hates sin and judges it, yet when He looks at us, He looks with compassion, for He realizes we are but dust. David continued with the Psalm saying, "As for man, his days are as grass: as a flower of the field, so he flourisheth. For the wind passeth over it, and it is gone; and the place thereof shall know it no more. But the mercy of the Lord is from everlasting to everlasting unto them that fear him, and his righteousness unto children's children" (vv. 15-17).

These were some of the expressions of David in the face of his sin. He realized the awful consequences of his own sins upon others and this brought brokenness of heart to him. Why should others suffer because of his sin? He prayed and wept for seven days when his little son suffered for his, David's sin.

On another occasion he went before the Lord when Israel was suffering and asked God why He was punishing them for his sin of numbering the people. When David was confronted by his sins of doubt and backsliding and other kinds of sins, he would find a place where he could meet God in quietness and establish himself again in the Lord. When convicted of his sin, he was a brokenhearted man before God and contrite in spirit.

A careful reading of Psalm 51 will show that because of his personal relationship to the Lord David could feel in part, at least, how God was hurt by his sin. Do we realize how God is hurt as a result of our sin? How many children have, after sinning, felt the hurt they have brought to their parents? How many of us who are parents have been hurt when our children have gone wrong? How then must God feel when we sin, since He is absolutely pure and holy.

Notice also David's attitude toward chastisement. Here is where we can learn a great deal. When he fled from Jerusalem during the time of Absalom's rebellion, David humbled himself before the Lord and acknowledged that God had a right to chastise him. He looked upon the experience as one in which God would work in his heart and make a better man of him. Here again the word "wait" comes into the picture. He waited in two ways upon God. He waited for the time that God would bring him back again to the throne. But he also waited on God as a servant waits upon his master. David put himself completely at God's disposal.

Finally, there was David's reaction to God's expressed purpose of seeing to it that there always would be someone of David's lineage on the throne. God made with him an everlasting covenant when He said, "And when thy days be fulfilled, and thou shalt sleep with thy fathers, I will set up thy seed after thee, which shall proceed out of thy bowels, and I will establish his kingdom. He shall build an house for my name, and I will establish the throne of his kingdom for ever" (II Sam. 7:12,13). God also promised that He would have mercy on David's seed and would never completely blot them out. This promise included Christ coming from the family of David. David's reaction was, "Who am I, O Lord God? and what is my house, that thou hast brought me hitherto?" He is still the same unspoiled, humble servant of God he was as a youth. In gratitude he said to God, "For thy word's sake, and according to thine own heart, hast thou done all these great things, to make thy servant know them" (II Sam. 7:21).

The final attitude of his heart is expressed in the following verses: "And now, O Lord God, the word that thou hast spoken concerning thy servant, and concerning his house, establish it for ever, and do as thou hast said. And let thy name be magnified for ever, saying, The Lord of hosts is the God over Israel: and let the house of thy servant David be established before thee. For thou, O Lord of hosts, God of Israel, hast revealed to thy servant, saying, I will build thee an house: therefore hath thy servant found in his heart to pray this prayer unto thee. And now, O Lord God, thou art that God, and thy words be true, and thou hast promised this goodness unto thy servant: Therefore now let it please thee to bless the house of thy servant, that it may continue for ever before thee: for thou, O Lord God, hast spoken it: and with thy blessing let the house of thy servant be blessed for ever" (II Sam. 7:25-29). David submitted himself to God and said in effect, "Lord, I will do what you want me to do." He put himself at God's disposal so that God could do and prosper His own name in any way that pleased Him. David recognized his own unworthiness—but humbly put himself at God's disposal so that God might fulfill His will. Like Paul, David knew that in himself was no good thing. David also learned the truth Paul so wonderfully expressed centuries later: "I can do all things through Christ which strengtheneth me."

Do we realize that we have been called of God to be co-heirs with Christ and to sit on the throne with Him, not just in eternity, not just sometime in the future, but NOW! We can enthrone Him in our hearts and live victoriously. This can only be as we hold the same attitude David did. Let us commit ourselves to Him and say, "Lord, work it out in me. Work it out today!"

Let us enthrone God in our hearts from now on and forever.

APPENDIX

HISTORICAL BACKGROUND OF PSALMS WRITTEN BY DAVID

There are some 73 Psalms accredited to David's authorship, the Holy Spirit, of course, being the Divine Author. These Psalms arose out of David's life experiences and God's dealing with his heart. Only those are listed here whose historical background we are reasonably sure of.

Psalm 3

A Psalm written by David when he fled from Absalom his son. See II Samuel, chapters 15-18.

Psalm 4

Another Psalm of David written when he fled from Absalom. See II Samuel, chapters 15-18.

Psalm 7

David defended himself against the slanderous charges of Cush during the time Saul hunted David, from place to place. See I Samuel chapters 24-26; especially I Samuel 24:9 and 26:19.

Psalm 11

David at Saul's court is advised to flee. See I Samuel, chapters 18, 19.

Psalm 15

The removal of the Ark of the Covenant to Zion. See II Samuel 6:12-19.

Psalm 18

Praise to God for deliverance from Saul and all other enemies. See II Samuel, chapter 22.

Psalm 21

This is a Psalm of praise for victory and though the historical occasion is not known, verses 3-6 remind us of II Samuel 7. An element in both the Psalm and the chapter point forward to Christ.

Psalm 23

Undoubtedly this spiritual treasure finds its background in David's experiences as a shepherd.

Psalm 24

This has to do with the inauguration of the newly captured fortress of Zion and the placing of the Ark in Jerusalem. See II Samuel, chapter 6.

Psalm 26

This is one of a number of Psalms in which David is found defending himself against false accusers. The particular occasion that called forth this Psalm is not known.

Psalm 27

This is a Psalm of faith and fear. Some believe that verse 10 has a reference to David's parents moving to Moab, and possibly dying there later. See I Samuel 22:1-4.

Psalm 30

David's gratitude at the dedication of his house. See II Samuel 5:11 and 7:2.

Psalm 32

This deals with the way of blessedness and forgiveness. It was possibly composed about the same time as Psalm 51, and for the same reason. See II Samuel, chapters 11,12. It is one of the penitential Psalms, the others being 6, 35, 51, 102, 130 and 143.

David's thanksgiving for deliverance from Abimelech, called Achish in I Samuel, chapter 21.

Psalm 35

A call for help when David was hunted like a wild animal by his enemies. See I Samuel 24.

Psalm 38

This is the third of the penitential Psalms. It may be connected with the time of Absalom's rebellion, though of this we cannot be sure. See II Samuel, chapters 15-18.

Psalm 39

Here is trust in trial. The historical background may be that of Absalom's rebellion. See II Samuel, chapters 15-18.

Psalm 40

David looks back on the period covering his accession to the throne and then to the problem of Absalom's rebellion. See II Samuel, chapters 2, 5, 15-18.

Psalm 41

It is thought that David became ill first because of his great sin and then because of his great sorrow in losing his infant son. This might account for Absalom's implication that David was failing in his duties as king (II Sam. 15:3). See also II Samuel, chapters 11-16 with Psalms 32 and 51.

Psalm 51

This is the fourth of the penitential Psalms. In it David expresses sorrow for sin and his repentance after committing the sins of adultery and murder. See II Samuel, chapters 11,12 and Psalm 32.

Psalm 52

Doeg, the Edomite, told Saul that David had been helped by Ahimelech the priest. Doeg's purpose was not to help David, but to hurt him. See I Samuel, chapters 21,22.

Psalm 54

The treachery and oppression of the Ziphites who were members of David's own tribe of Judah. See I Samuel 23:19-23 and 26:1-3.

Psalm 55

This was David's song of oppression during Absalom's rebellion. See II Samuel, chapters 15-18.

Psalm 56

The title of this Psalm is, "When the Philistines took him [David] in Gath." The historical background is found in I Samuel 21:10-15. Read also Psalm 34.

Psalm 57

David tells of his faith as a fugitive when he fled from Saul in the cave. The Scripture background is either I Samuel 22 or I Samuel 24.

Psalm 59

The time when Saul sent his soldiers to watch David's house with orders to put him to death. See I Samuel 19:11-18.

Psalm 60

While David fought the Syrians in the northeast, Edom invaded Palestine in the southeast and David sent Joab to repel them. It is thought this Psalm was written between these great battles. See II Samuel 10:6,16; II Chronicles 18:12,25; II Samuel 8:13,14; I Kings 11:15,16; I Chronicles 18:12,13.

Psalm 61

David's flight from Absalom. See II Samuel 18.

Psalm 62

David waits on God during the time of Absalom's rebellion. See II Samuel 18.

Psalm 63

David composed this song of satisfaction while in the wilderness of Judah during Absalom's rebellion. See II Samuel 18.

Psalm 64

This deals with the hurtful tongue and could fit two outstanding periods in David's life: the time when Doeg reported on David's visit to Ahimelech, and when Ahithophel turned traitor and went over to Absalom's side. In connection with Doeg see Psalm 52 and I Samuel 22. For information on Ahithophel read Psalm 55 and II Samuel, chapters 15-17.

Psalm 101

Written concerning the occasion when David decided to remove the ark to Jerusalem. See II Samuel 6:1-15.

Psalm 109

It may have as its background the satanically inspired persecution of David by Saul.

Psalm 131

This Psalm is thought to express David's attitude when he ascended the throne of Israel. See II Samuel 5:1-5, and I Chronicles 11:1-3.

Psalm 133

Here the unity of the tribes is dealt with at David's return after Absalom's rebellion. See II Samuel 5:1; I Chronicles 12:38-40; and II Samuel 19:14.

Psalm 140

Here is a cry for deliverance. Such men as Doeg, Absalom, and Ahithophel were the kind of enemies dealt with here. See II Samuel, chapters 22,23.

Psalm 142

This finds the Psalmist close to despair during his experience in the cave of Adulum in Engedi. See I Samuel, chapters 22,24.

Psalm 143

The Psalmist is in very deep distress and could have written these words when Absalom was pursuing him. See II Samuel, chapters 15-18.